THE SILVER LINING

The Silver Lining

Messages of Hope and Cheer

BY

JOHN H. JOWETT

CURIOSMITH

MINNEAPOLIS

Published by Curiosmith.
Minneapolis, Minnesota.
Internet: curiosmith.com.

Previously published by FLEMING H. REVELL CO. in 1907.

Supplementary content, book layout, and cover design:
Copyright © 2016 Charles J. Doe

ISBN 9781941281734

CONTENTS

1. UNDER THE FIG-TREE . . . 7

2. IN TIME OF FLOOD . . . 12

3. DIVINE AMELIORATIVES . . . 17

4. THE CURE FOR CARE . . . 22

5. PREPARING FOR EMERGENCIES . . . 26

6. "SILENT UNTO GOD" . . . 31

7. MY STRENGTH AND MY SONG! . . . 36

8. THE ABIDING COMPANIONSHIP . . . 41

9. LIGHT ALL THE WAY . . . 47

10. OUR BRILLIANT MOMENTS . . . 51

11. THE LORD'S GUESTS . . . 56

12. HIDDEN MANNA . . . 63

13. THE REJOICING DESERT . . . 67

14. THE TRANSFORMATION OF THE GRAVEYARD . . . 72

15. COMFORTED IN ORDER TO COMFORT . . . 77

16. THE MINISTRY OF HOPE . . . 82

17. LIFE WITH WINGS . . . 88

18. THE UNEXPECTED ANSWER . . . 92

19. THE CENSER AND THE SACRIFICE . . . 97

20. THE SCHOOL OF CHRIST . . . 103

21. THE MINISTRY OF REST . . . 108

22. WEALTH THAT NEVER FAILS . . . 113

23. THE DIVINE ABILITY . . . 120

24. NEW STRENGTH FOR COMMON TASKS . . . 125

25. THE MINISTRY OF THE CLOUD . . . 131

26. THE REALMS OF THE BLEST . . . 137

Chapter 1

UNDER THE FIG-TREE

When thou wast under the fig-tree I saw thee.—JOHN 1:48.

W hen thou wast under the fig-tree I saw thee." But was there any special significance in this? There must have been something of very deep significance, for it inspired Nathaniel to an outburst of joyful faith: "Thou art the Son of God."[1] Perhaps there was something in the tone in which the words were spoken; for revelations are not always contained in the literal words, they are often found in the way in which they are spoken. It is possible to say to a sorrowful and mourning widow, "I saw you," and the words will suggest nothing more than bare recognition; and one may use the same phrase and it would be weighted with warm and helpful sympathy. There was surely something in the tone of the Master which called forth the exuberant response of Nathaniel's heart. But there was more than this. "Under the fig-tree," was a phrase which recalled a deep and personal experience. Nathaniel had been in the habit of retiring in the shade of the fig-tree, away from the crowd, and away from his labor, depressed by feelings of saddened loneliness and alienation. His was a chaste and sensitive soul, and there was much in his day to fill his delicate spirit with despondency and pain. So he was often found apart, under the fig-tree. The neighbors thought him moody; in reality he was thoughtful. He was described as dreamy; in reality he was prayerful. Sometimes he was esteemed a little proud; in reality he bore the burden of oppressive sadness.

---

1 Matthew 16:16.

He used to retire into the quiet garden, lock the gate, and under the fig-tree, with no one near, he would pour out his soul before God.

Can we exercise a prudent imagination, and attempt to realize Nathaniel's state? I think he was probably *burdened in worship*. He felt his spirit fettered by the multitudinous rules and regulations which had gathered round about the acts and offices of worship. He sought to be punctilious in their observation, but he labored under the heavy load. A certain amount of harness is helpful to a beast; it directs and concentrates his strength at the needful points, and makes the yoke tolerable and easy. But it is possible so to multiply the harness that it adds to the burden, rather than reduces it. And rules and regulations can be helpful to the movements of the spirit, but if they are multiplied they increase its strain. In Nathaniel's day the rules and regulations had increased until every natural move-ment was harassed and irritated, and life became a galling bondage. Nathaniel hungered for free intimacy, for the emancipation of a friendly walk with God. And then I think he was *weary in service*. The attempts to do good seemed so fruitless in their issues. The streets of town and village rang with hypocrisy and vice, and his own little efforts appeared to have no more purifying influence than the dropping of white snowflakes into an open sewer.

And then, too, I think he was *faint in waiting*. The promised deliverer was long in coming. He looked out with aching, weary eyes, but the emancipator did not appear. And his spirit grew faint and desponding. There is nothing so exhausting as mere waiting. Work does not tire a man so much as the looking for work. The hour of labor speeds like a weaver's shuttle; the hour of waiting drags like a cumbersome load. How long the minutes seem when we are waiting for the doctor! The loved one is passing into deeper need, and we listen for the hand upon the latch. Every moment seems an age. And there were many in the time of Nathaniel who were "wait-ing for the doctor"; the general life was sick and diseased, and the great Physician had not yet come! And these men waited, looking for "the consolation of Israel"! And Nathaniel was one of the wait-ers, and in the long waiting he had grown faint. Is it any wonder, then, that this man, burdened in worship, weary in service, and faint in waiting, should often be found apart in the retirement of some secluded garden, under a fig-tree, with downcast and despondent spirit, looking wistfully towards heaven and God? "When thou wast under the fig-tree I saw thee."

"I saw thee." And how much the seeing means! The phrase has infinitely more significance than that of bare recognition. It is not only that Nathaniel was noticed; it means that he was understood. Our Lord's sight is insight. The majority of us see, but only a few perceive. "See ye, indeed, but perceive not."[1] We see a sign, but we cannot give it an interpretation. We see a wrinkle, a grey hair, a tear, a smile, a look of care, a bent back, but we do not perceive their spiritual significance. Our Master not only sees; He "in-sees." When He looked at Nathaniel He understood him. He interpreted his thoughts and fears. He saw him through and through. "He knew what was in man."[2] But the Master's seeing implies more than this. It is not only that sight was insight; His perceptions were compassions. He was "touched" with the feelings of men's infirmities. He did not bring to bear upon men the mere dry light of understanding; the light was warm and genial, and sunny with the grace of sympathy. The apostolic word is very beautiful, He was "touched." But the sight means even more than this. The understanding and the sympathy were joined to the ministry of cooperation. The Master not only feels, He works; He not only sympathizes, He serves. When He saw Nathaniel under the fig-tree, His understanding, His sympathy, His power, all combined in a ministry of benevolent and beneficent love.

Here, then, is the evangel. Our Lord sees us when we are under the gloom of the fig-tree, when in sadness and weariness we are turning tired eyes at the expectancy of help. "Before that Philip called thee," before he came out into the open, when he was half hidden, when his soul-life was secret and unconfessed, when in grave despondency he was turning his weary eyes toward heaven—"I saw thee." He sees and knows us *then.* He sees us in the gropings in the gloom. That is the glory of our Redeemer. Anybody can see an electric light, but to feel the current, when there is not enough to make a light, requires a more refined discernment. We all become aware

---

1 Isaiah 6:9.
2 John 2:25.

of the electrical power when there is enough to ring a bell; but when the power which is stored in the wires is feeble and faint, it requires something as sensitive as the palate to detect it. Our Master discerns the feeble stirrings of spiritual life. When there is not enough to illumine the soul, or to make its powers ring out the truth, He detects the faint beginnings which to other people are unknown. The woman of Samaria comes to Him. She was only a common woman of the city. Far from being a light, she was like a burnt-out fire. But I think that in her desolate soul there were often faint and uncertain movements. She had long seasons of despondency, with little flickerings of aspiration after a better life. I think she often went apart, and in deep dejection of spirit sighed out her woe. We are not told that our Master spake to her of these seasons, and yet I cannot but think He did. He would mention one place and another place, and one thing and another thing, which would recall to her the experiences of these darker seasons. "When thou wast under the fig-tree I saw thee!" One after another the deepest things in her life were recalled to her, until at length she turned away to her friends, saying, "Come, see a man who told me all the things that ever I did."[1]

And was it not so with Zacchaeus? Can we think that when Jesus looked up at Zacchaeus and bade him come and offer hospitality, it was the first time He had seen him? Nay, I think He had often passed him in the streets, He had seen the shadow over his face. There was unrest and trouble in his eye. He looked like a man who was often awake at nights. For Zacchaeus often went home with a full purse and a very empty and impoverished heart. He was often "under the fig-tree," in gloom and despondency, casting fitful glances at the better life. And so when the Master called to him, there was something in the very tone which revealed that he was understood. We are not told what they talked about on their way to the publican's house, but I think I can hear the Master saying to His newly-found disciple, "when thou wast under the fig-tree I saw thee." I say this is the way of the Master. He sees us in the faint beginning and gropings of the spiritual life. "When he was yet *a long way off* his father saw him!"[2] That is characteristic of the Divine eyes. He sees us in the

1 John 4:29.
2 Luke 15:20.

long distance! The first faint impulses are recognized; the first turning is known. When we are under the fig-tree He sees us!

This, surely, is a word full of heartening and inspiration. We
are never alone. Our Saviour understands us, sympathizes with
us, cooperates with us. He is with us under the fig-tree! And see
how rich and wealthy is the promise. "Hereafter ye shall see heaven
opened and the angels of God ascending and descending on the Son
of Man."[1] How glorious and fitting is the issue! Nathaniel is to see
heaven opened! The man who has been in the gloom of the fig-tree,
with fitful and uncertain glimpses through the broken clouds, is to
attain to firm, clear, and permanent vision. And the man who is so
frequently timid, and wonders at the controlling power of life and
the world, is to have his confidence steadied and stayed, and is to be
made sure of the sovereignty of Christ.

---

1 John 1:51.

Chapter 2

IN TIME OF FLOOD

When the enemy shall come in like a flood, the Spirit of the Lord shall lift up a standard against him.—Isaiah 59:19.

These heartening words were spoken to exiles who were preparing to return to the homeland. They had become so accustomed to their captivity that emancipation seemed a dream. Even when they lifted their eyes to the possibilities of return they seemed to gaze upon range after range of accumulating difficulties which would obstruct their journey home. As often as the prophet proclaimed their deliverance they proclaimed their fears. Their fears were laid one by one, but as soon as one was laid another arose!

There was, for example, the wilderness to be crossed with all its fierce and sombre desolation! "The wilderness shall rejoice and blossom as the rose."[1] And there was the weary, pathless desert, offering only the prospect of homelessness to the bewildered pilgrim! "And an highway shall be there, and a way,"[2] clean and clear across it. There are waters to be crossed and floods to be overcome! "When thou passest through the waters they shall not overflow thee."[3] And other difficulties will arise, all the more burdensome because unforeseen! "Every valley shall be exalted, and every mountain and hill shall be brought low."[4] And the enemies on the right hand and the left hand,

---

1 Isaiah 35:1.
2 See Isaiah 35:8.
3 See Isaiah 43:2.
4 Isaiah 40:4.

what about them? The hostile peoples will accept their chance, and will come down upon the returning company in destructive array! "When the enemy shall come in like a flood, the Spirit of the Lord shall lift up a standard against him."[1] To every fear the prophet presents a promise; to every suspicion he offers an assurance. Now, we, too, are exiles returning to the homeland. We, too, have been in the dark realms of captivity, and by His redeeming grace our eyes have been lifted toward the better country. And we, too, are full of uncertainties and fears. There is a desert to traverse, a wilderness to cross, waters to pass through, mountains to climb, and we know not how we may safely reach our journey's end. And particularly are we beset by the enemy, who suddenly and unexpectedly sweeps down upon our path. But if we have the fears, ours, too, are the promises. Between the enemy and ourselves there shall be erected the standard of the Lord. "When the enemy shall come in like a flood, the Spirit of the Lord shall lift up a standard against him."

"When the enemy shall come in like a *flood.*" I think that the figure is surely taken from the river-beds of their native land. They had looked upon the dry, bleached ravines in time of drought, when scarcely a rivulet lisped down its rocky course. And then the rain had fallen on the hills, or the snow had melted upon the distant mountains, and the waters had torn down like a flood. I have picnicked away up in the solitudes of the higher Tees, when there was only a handful of water passing along, a little stream which even a child could cross. And once I saw what the natives call the "roll" coming away in the distance. Great rains had fallen upon the heights, and this was their issue; in a moment the quiet stream became a roaring torrent, and shouted along in thunderous flood. That, I think, is the figure of my text. When the sudden "roll" shall come in the life, and the little rivulet is changed into tempestuous waters, "When the enemy shall come in like a flood, the Spirit of the Lord shall lift up a standard against him."

Now, what are some of these flood times in life when the enemy comes against us in overwhelming power? There is the flood of *passion.* There are many among my readers who do not know that flood. We are very differently constituted, and some there are in

---

1 Isaiah 59:19.

whom these particular waters bring no peril. There are some whose passion fills up slowly like a cistern; there are others who overflow in a moment. There are some who are constitutionally calm; there are others who "boil" at the slightest provocation. Well, now, floods always destroy something valuable and beautiful. I have watched a great river in flood, and I have seen how many precious things are carried down in the violent stream; a sheep that has been harmlessly playing by the bank, some tender sapling, some useful bridge. And so it is with the flood of passion that sweeps through the soul. It always damages the life through which it flows. Some seed of the kingdom, just beginning to germinate, is washed out of the ground. Some tender growth is impaired or destroyed, some little plant of meekness, or gentleness, or faith, or hope, or love. Even onlookers can frequently see the ruin; and to the Lord the fruitful place must become a desert. "The enemy has come in like a flood."

And sometimes the flood is in the form of a great *sorrow*, and we are engulfed by it. Billow after billow goes over us, and does tremendous damage. I know that there is a sorrow appointed of the Almighty, but it is never ordained to hurt or destroy. And yet how often this particular flood, rushing into a life, works havoc with spiritual things. Have we not known many such in our own experience? "Was not So-and-so at one time a great worker in the Church?" And the answer was, "Yes, but he has never done anything since his child died!" The flood had done its evil work. And so it frequently is in lives that have been drowned in the enveloping waters. In one of our churches a little while ago a flood occurred, and the two things that were injured were the heating apparatus and the organ. I could not but think of the destructiveness wrought in the soul by the gathering waters of sorrow. Very frequently they put out the fires of geniality, and they silence the music and the song.

And so it is, one may say, with all the perilous waters that arise in human life. Sometimes the flood gathers from a multitudinous contribution of petty cares. It is amazing how mighty a volume can be made with small contributions. We could deal with one; the multitude overwhelms us! We could deal with one worry, but multitudes of them create the flood we call anxiety, and we are over-thrown. And again great damage is done, working havoc to our peace and self-control and magnanimity.

Now, whenever a flood in the life damages a life the work is the work of the devil. When I am tempted into overflowing passion, or into excessive sorrow, or into overwhelming care, it is the work of the enemy. I think that if we could realize this we should be greatly helped in these perilous and frequently recurring seasons. If we could only practice our eyes so as to see in the tempting circumstance the face of the evil one we should be less inclined to the snare. If we could only get into our minds and hearts the settled conviction that behind all these threatening approaches there is the ugly enemy of our souls, we should more eagerly turn our eyes and feet toward the Lord of life and beauty. Now that Lord of life offers Himself as our defense in the time of the rising flood. He will "lift up a standard against him." I think that is very beautiful! King Canute had his regal chair carried down to the flowing tide, and he commanded the waters to retreat. The waters paid no heed, and the mighty flood advanced. But our King raises His standard against the threatening flood, and the retreat is absolutely ensured. In the moment when we are tempted to the overwhelming passion He will come between us and the flood. "The waters shall not overflow thee." Have you noticed that wonderfully suggestive passage in the Book of Revelation where a promise is made of help in the time of flood? "And the serpent cast out of his mouth water as a flood after the woman, that he might cause her to be carried away at the flood. And the earth helped the woman, and the earth opened her mouth, and swallowed up the flood which the dragon cast out of his mouth."[1] I believe that that great promise has been abundantly confirmed in countless lives. Even the earth itself is our ally in contending with the foe. The beauties of nature will help us to contend with the forces of evil desire. I believe that if we more frequently communed with the flowers of the field we should find that the earth was a minister of the Holy Spirit. The earth would swallow up the flood. But we have more than Nature as our defense; we have the Lord of nature, the Lord in nature, not so much the supernatural as the Spirit who pervades nature and all things. That gracious Spirit will subtly steal into the threatened parts of our life, and will contend with our foe.

---

1 Revelation 12:15–16.

And so, too, it is in the flood times of sorrow. The Spirit of the Lord will engage for us, "lest we be swallowed up with overmuch sorrow."[1] Have I not seen it done a hundred times? Have I not seen sorrow come into a life, and it has been entirely a minister of good and never of ill? The devil has not got hold of it, and used it as a destructive flood. Not one thing has been damaged or destroyed. It has been a minister of irrigation rather than destruction, and in the moist place of tears beautiful ferns have grown, the exquisite graces of compassion and long-suffering and peace.

"The Spirit of the Lord will lift up a standard!"[2] Well, then, let Him do it. Do not let us attempt to do it for ourselves. Let us hand it over to Him, "Undertake Thou for me, O Lord."[3] The life of faith just consists in a quiet, conscious, realizing trust in the all-willing and all-powerful Spirit of God.

---

1 2 Corinthians 2:7.
2 Isaiah 59:19.
3 See Isaiah 38:14.

Chapter 3

DIVINE AMELIORATIVES

Sleeping for sorrow.—LUKE 22:45.

am not concerned with the element of human weakness suggested by my text; I want to dwell entirely upon the Divine graciousness which I think is enshrined in it.

"Sleeping for sorrow." Is it not a very strange conjunction of words? One would have thought that wakefulness and sorrow would have been associated, and that sleep and sorrow would never have found communion. But here is sorrow passing into sleep! As though sorrow itself contains a gracious opiate which lulls and subdues into slumber. As though God had determined that every distress should carry a certain palliative in order that we might not be burdened beyond measure. When sorrow becomes very intense it induces sleep. A Divine ameliorative is at hand, and the strain of the galling burden is lightened. They say in the North that there is never a nettle that has not its companion dock. The dock supplies the opiate for relieving and destroying the sting of the nettle. And so I wish to consider some of these Divine amelioratives which the good Lord has appointed for reducing the burdensomeness of grief, and for making the daily sorrow tolerable.

The ameliorative of sleep. What a wonderful minister is the genius of sleep! When our bodies are tired out, and the nervous force is almost spent, and we feel ourselves wearied and "down," what a hotbed is provided for irritableness, and doubt, and despondency and despair! A tired-out body offers a fertile rootage to all manner of mental ailments. Many a man in the evening time feels that life is very colorless and juiceless, and this sense of the somberness and dullness arises from a body which has temporarily lost its spring. And then comes sleep! During the hours of sleep our gracious God comes and refills the exhausted lamp, and in the morning the touchiness and irritableness and tastelessness have all gone, and we face the new day as men renewed. The Lord has been near with His gracious palliative of sleep, and the oppressiveness of the passing day has been removed.

Then how frequently sleep acts as a gracious opiate when we are inclined to make precipitate vows! Something has happened and we hastily resolve upon hasty action. But some discreet friend says to us, "Sleep on it." And the influence of the one night's sleep scatters our rash resolve like morning mist. Have we not recently been told of a great minister who, in some moment of impatience, resolved upon sending his resignation to his deacons, but he took the counsel of his wife to "sleep on it," and the resignation was never sent. God's gracious gift came in the meantime, and the storm-tossed mind and heart were laid to rest.

And what a wonderful servant is this same sleep in the time of bereavement! I have frequently known a widow in the very first day of her widowhood, when the body of her husband was scarcely cold, pass into a deep and most refreshing sleep. "I have had the best night's sleep I have had for many a month," she has said; and this was the first night of bereavement! "Sleeping for sorrow." It is a wonderfully gracious providence of our God to mingle this Divine opiate with our sorrows, and to put us into a quiet and restoring sleep. "He giveth His beloved sleep."[1]

The ameliorative of Time. What a healing minister we have in Time itself. The old proverb tells us that Time brings roses. And a still older proverb, coming down from the days of the Romans, tells us that Time is generally the best doctor. The new railway cutting is a great red gash in the green countryside, but Time is a great healer and restorer, and day after day the bald, bare place is being re-covered with fern and grass and wild flower, until at length the ugly cutting harmonizes with the colors of the surrounding landscape, and the

1 Psalm 127:2.

gash is healed. And Time works a similar history with human life. A cutting injury is done to me. I think I can never forget it. The wound is deep, rankling is sore. But Time takes the thing in hand, and little by little, and day by day, the healing process is continued, until at length the open wound is closed, and I wonder how I could have been so silly as to make so much stir about it. And we all know what Time can do even for the sharp pangs of a great bereavement. In the first dark and cloudy day it seems as though no light will ever fall upon our path again. "I shall never laugh any more." Oh, yes, you will! Time, the Lord's ameliorative, will begin to minister to the broken spirit, and however incredible it may now appear, some day the smiles will come back in the blanched cheek, and the mouth will be filled with laughter. And this because, as the days go by, Time turns a beautiful memory into an alluring hope. We not only feel the season behind us, but the pulling power of the age that lies before. Let us never forget, when we are counting our blessings, to thank God for the glorious ministry of gracious Time.

The Divine ameliorative of work. May we not speak of work as one of the Lord's servants appointed by Him to subdue the distresses of life, and to mitigate its pangs? How frequently it happens that the needful work that is required to be done immediately after a death is a gracious helpmeet to the spirit. We have to be busy about the funeral, and even that bit of business is a minister of rest. We say one of another, "It's well she had so much to do." Goethe's mother said of her son, "My son, when he has a grief, puts it in a poem and so gets rid of it." We cannot all put our griefs into poems, but it is amazing how much of them we can put into work. And so it is well for us to look upon work as a signal token of Divine Providence and Fatherly love and grace. He has appointed us to work, and the work has been ordained for our eternal good. "Cursed is the ground for thy sake"; yes, but the cursing of the ground was for the blessedness of man. In cursing the ground God blessed the race. When God cursed the ground He made it essential that man should work. The curse was only a restraining of the natural energies of the earth, in order that man should cooperate and bring the hidden things to fruition. God made work compulsory in order that man might regain his lost Eden. To lose his Eden, and then to have no work, would have made the alienation too grievous to be borne. The compulsory work was the decree of Eternal love.

I am not surprised, therefore, when I turn to the New Testament to find how great was Paul's fear of indolent Christians. The early believers gave up their ordinary work and passively waited the coming of their Lord. Now Paul knew that, in the time of stress, and persecution, and tribulation, to have no work would be to take sides with the enemy. Therefore "let every man abide in the calling wherein he was called."[1] Let every man go on working, for he will find in his work an ameliorative for his sorrows. To cast aside work is to deprive oneself of the means of grace. A doctor, quite recently in my hearing, said to a man who was inclined to become a little morbid and depressed, "Go out and weed your garden." The weeding of the garden was the smallest part of the hour's work; while the man was weeding the garden he was also extracting weeds from his own heart and life. Let us thank God for work.

The Divine ameliorative of service. I distinguish between work and service. Work is primarily for our own profit; service is primarily profit for others. And therefore I speak now of labor expended in another's good, and in this kind of service I say there is a grand ameliorative for the griefs and distresses of life. It is an amazing thing to watch the new color which our sorrow assumes when we go out to minister to others. The rawness goes out of our own wound while we are dressing the wounds of our neighbor. Our own pang is lessened when we seek to take the pang out of another's soul. "I felt as though my heart would break, so I just got up and went out to help a poor body who I knew was in need." Yes, and while she went to bring comfort to her needy sister the heart's-ease came into her own soul. This is the beautiful, gracious way of God. We can go out with a broken heart to minister to other broken hearts, and a cooling balm is applied to our own feverish pain and fears. Along these lines we can all make bold and immediate experiment, and you may depend upon it you will find that in this kind of service there is hidden a gracious opiate which deadens the sense of our own sorrows and makes it possible for us to endure them.

All these are Divine amelidratives, the gracious ministers of

---

1 1 Corinthians 7:20.

God, and I would that we might more frequently remember them when we seek to tell the story of His mercy and grace. Let us think of them as the angels of the Lord, appointed by Him to do us service in the dark and cloudy day. "He shall give His angels charge concerning thee, to keep thee in all thy ways."[1]

1 Psalm 91:11.

Chapter 4

THE CURE FOR CARE

Fret not thyself.—PSALM 37:1.

"*Fret not thyself,*" Do not get into a perilous heat about things. And yet, if ever heat were justified, it was surely justified in the circumstances outlined in the psalm. Evildoers were moving about clothed in purple and fine linen, and faring sumptuously every day. "Workers of iniquity" were climbing into the supreme places of power, and were tyrannizing over their less fortunate brethren. Sinful men and women were stalking through the land in the pride of life, and basking in the light and comfort of great prosperity. And good men were becoming heated and fretful. "Fret not thyself." Do not get unduly heated! Keep cool! Even in a good cause fretfulness is not a wise helpmeet. Fretting only heats the bearings, it does not generate the steam. It is no help to a train for the axles to get hot; their heat is only a hindrance; the best contribution which the axles can make to the progress of the train is to keep cool. Fretfulness is just the heating of the axles; it is heat in the wrong place; it is heat become a source of weakness rather than strength. We sometimes say of a man, concerning his relationship to some particular topic, "He got quite hot over it!" That kind of heat does not increase a man's driving power, not does it contribute to his vindication. It is only the perilous heat of the axles.

Now, when the axles get heated it is because of unnecessary friction; dry surfaces are grinding together which ought to be kept in smooth cooperation by a delicate cushion of oil. And is it not a suggestive fact that this word "fret" is closely akin to the word "friction," and is indicative of the absence of the anointing oil of the grace of God? In fretfulness, thought is grinding against thought, desire against desire, will against will; a little bit of grit gets into the bearings—some slight disappointment, some ingratitude, some discourtesy, and the smooth working of the life is checked. Friction begets heat, and with the heat most dangerous conditions are created.

We can never really foresee to what kind of disaster this perilous heat may lead. The psalmist, in the early verses of this psalm, points out some of the stages of increasing destructiveness to which this unclean fire assuredly leads. It is somewhat strange, and yet not strange, that the second piece of counsel in this psalm is concerned with the disposition of envy. It is not put there as an irrelevance. It indicates a possible succession. Fretfulness frequently leads to jealousy. For what is jealousy? Again, let it be said that jealousy is heat out of place. The "jealous" man and the "zealous" man are somewhat akin, but in one case the fire is clean and in the other it is unclean. It is the difference between fervor and fever. Fretfulness creates the unclean fire of envy. Now see the further stage proclaimed by the Psalmist. *"Cease from anger."* The fire is now burning furiously, noisy in the fierceness of its wrath. What shall we expect as the climax of all this? *"Fret not thyself in any wise to do evil."* That is what I should expect. Men who have worked themselves into envy and anger will be led into the very evil they originally resented. Men begin by fretting "because of evildoers," and they end by "doing the evil" themselves. "Behold how great a matter a little fire kindleth!"[1] "Fret not thyself!" Do not let thy bearings get hot. Let the oil of the Lord keep thee cool, lest by reason of an unclean heat thou be reckoned among the evildoers.

How, then, is fretfulness to be cured? The Psalmist brings in the heavenly to correct the earthly. This psalm is full of "the Lord"! "The Lord" is the refrain of almost every verse, as though it were only in the power of the heavenly that this dangerous fire could be subdued. Let us look at the counsel in detail.

"Trust in the Lord." "Trust." It is, perhaps, helpful to remember

---

1 James 3:5.

that the word which is here translated "trust" is elsewhere in the Old
Testament translated "careless." "Be careless in the Lord!" Instead
of carrying a load of care let care be absent! It is the carelessness
of little children running about the house in the assurance of their
father's providence and love. It is the singing disposition that leaves
something for the parent to do. Assume that He is working as well
as thyself, and working even when things appear to be adverse.

I remember meeting a man in Birmingham, not so very long
ago, a man who is honestly and earnestly seeking to live a Christian
life, but he mourned to me the depression under which he was suffering on that particular day. "I feel very depressed; my feelings are
gloomy; I feel as though my Lord were far away!" It was a very mis-
erable morning; the unclean snow was melting in the streets, and
a November fog possessed the town. I said to him, "Do you think
the Welsh water is running into our town today? Has the supply
from the Welsh hills been stopped? The day is gloomy enough, the
fog is about, and the atmosphere is certainly chilly, but the water
from the Welsh hills is flowing into the city quite as abundantly as
it will do on the sunniest day in June! The fog in Birmingham will
not check the gracious supply from the hills!" And so it is with our
feelings. The supply of grace is not determined by the changes in
our moods; it is independent of our feelings. "There is a river the
streams whereof shall make glad the city of God!" That river is flowing even when we are temporarily depressed, and we are no longer
enjoying the ecstasy of the heights. "Trust in the Lord!" Believe in
His fidelity! Assume that the river is flowing even on the darkest
day. This would be an amazing cure for fretfulness and excessive
care.

"Delight thyself also in the Lord."[1] How beautiful the phrase!
The literal significance is this, "Seek for delicacies in the Lord." Yes,
and if we only set about with ardent purpose to discover the delicacies of the Lord's table, we should have no time and no inclination
to fret. But this is just what the majority of us do not do. We take
the crumbs from the Master's table, and we have no taste of the
excellent delicacies. Now the delicacies of anything are not found
in the elementary stages; we have to move forward to the advanced.

---

1 Psalm 37:4.

The delicacies of music are not found in the first half-dozen lessons; it is only in the later stages that we come to the exquisite. And so it is in art, and so it is in literature, and so it is with the "things of the Lord." "Eye hath not seen, nor ear heard, neither have entered into the heart of man, the things which God hath prepared for them that love Him."[1] Let us be ambitious for the excellent! God has not yet given to us of His best. He always keeps the best wine until the last. We shall never reach God's superlative! The "unsearchable riches of Christ" will reveal themselves more and more to us throughout the glorious seasons of the eternal day. When we sit at the table of the Lord, tasting of His delicacies, fretfulness will be unable to breathe.

"Commit thy way unto the Lord."[2] "Thy way!" What is that? Any pure purpose, any worthy ambition, any duty, anything we have got to do, any road we have got to tread, all our outgoings. "Commit thy way unto the Lord." Commit it to Him, not merely when we are in the middle of the way and are stuck and lost in the mire. Let us commit our beginnings unto Him, before we have gone wrong; let us have His companionship from the very outset of the journey. "I am Alpha." He likes to be in at our beginnings. What am I purposing for tomorrow? What am I setting out to do? Have I committed it to the Lord, or am I setting out upon a solitary journey? If I am going out alone, fretfulness will encounter me before I have gone many steps in the way; if I go out in the company of Jesus I shall have the peace that passeth understanding, and the heat of my life will be the ardor of an intense devotion.

"Rest in the Lord."[3] Having done all this, and doing it all, trusting in the Lord, delighting in the Lord, committing my way unto the Lord, let me now just "rest." Don't worry. Whatever happens, just refer it to the Lord! If it be anything injurious He will suppress it. If it be anything containing helpful ministry He will adapt it to our need. This is the cure for care.

---

1 1 Corinthians 2:9.

2 Psalm 37:5.

3 Psalm 37:7.

Chapter 5

PREPARING FOR EMERGENCIES

Before governors and kings shall ye be brought for My sake, for a testimony to them and to the Gentiles. But when they deliver you up, be not anxious how or what ye shall speak; for it shall be given you in that hour what ye shall speak. For it is not ye that speak, but the Spirit of your Father that speaketh in you.—Matthew 10:18–20 (R. V.).

Ye shall be brought before governors and kings." This was said to fishermen who had lived a quiet, unobtrusive life on and by the Galilean lake. It does not require much imagination to enter into the panic occasioned by the Master's words. In our day, to appear before a Court even as a plaintiff makes one limp and weak and useless; to appear as defendant is to suffer collapse. And these humble, toiling men, with their horny hands, with their homely dialect, are told that they must appear before kings and governors to answer for their lives! It is no easy experience for obscure people to appear in the presence of the great and mighty. They are often either the victims of awkwardness or the prey of paralyzing fear. They do the wrong thing; they say the wrong thing; things they purposed saying and doing are forgotten; both in the presence of the august and when they leave it they feel abashed and ashamed. If not the prey of awkwardness they are in the bondage of fear; the pith goes out of their powers, and they feel as though their wills are melting away. It was by no means an easy prospect which the Master held out before them. "Ye shall be brought before governors and kings." When they heard the words their secret hearts began to busy themselves with this unspoken question: "What shall we do?" Immediately they became anxious, possessed by worry, thrown into mental and spiritual disorder.

Here, then, are the disciples contemplating a remote emergency. The emergency will come. It is inevitable. The line of their life, at present commonplace and even, will rise into a great crisis. As sure as the morrow comes the emergency will come with it! What shall they do? That was the pregnant question, and the question suggests our present meditation. How shall we prepare for emergencies?

Our life now may be a level, regular road; but tomorrow the character of the road will be changed, and we shall be confronted by some great and unusual task. What shall we do? It may not be ours to stand as culprits before powers of an imperial or ecclesiastical kind. But it is not only kings and governors who make life's crises. There are presences and powers of another kind, great, strong, and inevitable. Other things may stop us, arrest us, imprison us in close bondage. There are other kings beside those who sit on thrones. Tomorrow I may not stand before a king who wears the purple, but I may come into the presence of sickness. I may approach the sudden shadow of calamity. I may come within the chill and loneliness of bereavement. I may meet King Death himself, the king of kings, the king of terror, the shadow feared of man. "Ye shall be brought before" sickness, calamity, bereavement, death! These presences are inevitable. What shall we do? How shall we prepare for them?

"Ye shall be brought before kings." When the disciples heard the words many of them began already to prepare the words which they would address to the king. "No," said the Master, "do not prepare a speech, be not anxious what ye shall speak. Don't prepare a speech, prepare yourselves!" That is the way to meet all emergencies. Not to make little detailed arrangements and little specified plans and finished speeches, but to have our souls in health and to meet all emergencies with the invincibility of a prepared life.

"Be not anxious." The first step in all wise preparation for emergencies is to cultivate the strength of stillness. Anxiety is mental and spiritual unrest. It always signifies the absence of stillness, the calmness which is the very secret of strength.

Most of us are familiar with the calm people to whom we

instinctively turn in times of stress and danger. Among the poor
and the working classes, where neighborliness is more alive than
among the well-to-do, it is beautiful how some one neighbor is
renowned for this quality of calmness. There is nearly always some
woman in the locality to whom poor people turn when life passes
into the strain of some great emergency. She is sent for in cases of
accident, or when bad news is received, or when Death is at the
door. The neighbors say one to another, as their first and readiest
counsel, "Send for Mrs. So-and-So," and the calm woman comes
on the scene of general panic and disorder, and her presence at once
begins to restore confidence. She has the strength of stillness. What
do we mean by this calmness? We mean that she is self-possessed,
that she has everything in hand, that all her powers are at her disposal like the well-arranged tools in the carpenter's shop. We have a
very expressive word by which we describe this quality of mind. We
call it "collectedness." The opposite of collectedness is distraction,
when a man's powers do not work together, but one is passive and
another is active, one pulling this way and another that, and there
is no general aim and direction. The collected man has his faculties
about him like well-ordered troops, and he says to one "Go," and
he goeth, and to another "Come," and he cometh, and to all his
servants "Do this," and they do it. These are the people who save us
from the perils of panic, and turn our crises into advantage. Lord
Kitchener is known in the Army as the strong, silent man. There is
no flurry or hurry about him. He moves toward seeming disaster as
though he were going to a feast. None of his powers are paralysed by
disorder, none are impoverished by anxiety, no strength is wasted,
everything is intent upon a quietly seen and deliberate end. Now,
if we are to meet the crises of life, this calmness of spirit must be
cultivated. It is infinitely better than a prepared speech or a ready-
made plan; these may fail us when the crisis arrives; the stillness is
our friend in the dark and stormy day.

But if we are to obtain the strength of stillness we must practice the art of *living in the present*. "Be not anxious for tomorrow." "Sufficient for the day is the evil thereof."[1] We must not need-
lessly go out to anticipate the crisis. We must not meet our trouble

---

1 See Matthew 6:34.

half-way. Half-met troubles always appear monstrous. Anticipation makes trifles loom gigantic. The thing that frowns, in threatening and terrific guise, often ceases to terrify when we draw closer to it. I saw a picture some time ago which represented a rising storm. Seen at some little distance it appeared as though dark, black, threatening cloud-battalions were speedily covering the entire sky and blotting out all the patches of light and hope. But when I went a little nearer to the picture I found that the artist had subtly fashioned his clouds out of angel faces, and all these black battalions wore the winsome aspect of genial friends. I have had that experience more than once away from the realm of picture and fiction, in the hard ways of practical life. The clouds I feared and worried about, and concerning which I wasted so much precious strength, lost their frown and revealed themselves as my friends. Other clouds never arrived; they were purely imaginary, or they melted away before they reached my threshold. "Be not anxious for tomorrow." Live in the immediate moment. Practice the art of omission. Leave out some things and concentrate upon the rest. The best preparation for the morrow is quiet attention today.

> I ask Thee for a present mind,
> Intent on pleasing Thee.[1]

If I am to be a capable expert, living in the present, I must engage in the *practice of trusting God* in every passing moment of my life. What is this that is nearest to me? What is this duty? What is this task? What is this immediate trouble? Just here and just now let me trust in God. Let me turn this present moment into happy confidence, and in this very season let me hold communion with my God. Let my trust be deliberate, repeatedly deliberate, until by conscious, volitional trust I come to have instinctive confidence in my God. Let me fill the present with holy faith, and "the changes that will surely come I shall not fear to see."

And why shall I not fear them? *"Be not anxious how or what ye shall speak: for it is not ye that speak, but the spirit of your Father that speaketh in you."* Lay hold of the last two words of this great

---

1 A quote from *Father, I Know that All My Life* by Anna L. Waring.

promise, "in you." That is the secret of everything. Every act of trust increases your capacity for God. Every time I trust Him I have more room for Him. He dwells within me in ever-richer fullness, occupying room after room in my life. That is a glorious assurance, and one that is filled with infinite comfort. Let me repeat it again, for it is the very music of the soul; little acts of trust make larger room for God. In my trifles I can prepare for emergencies. Along a commonplace road I can get ready for the hill. In the green pastures and by the still waters I can prepare myself for the valley of the shadow. For when I reach the hill, the shadow, the emergency, I shall be God-possessed: He will dwell in me. And where He dwells He controls. If He lives in my life He will direct my powers. It will not be I that speak, but my Father that speaketh in me. He will govern my speech. He will empower my will. He will enlighten my mind. He will energize and vitalize my entire life.

Here, then, is the little sequence I have been endeavoring to unfold. Put your trust in the Lord and you will live well in the immediate present; live well in the immediate present and you will have the spirit of calmness which is the secret of strength. The emergency will not affright you. You will approach it with that quietness which is the essential factor in triumph.

Chapter 6

"SILENT UNTO GOD"

My soul, wait thou only upon God; for my expectation is from Him.
He only is my rock and my salvation; He is my defense; I shall not
be moved.—PSALM 62:5, 6.

M y soul!" Here is a man communing with his own soul! He is
deliberately addressing himself, and calling himself to attention. He is of set purpose breaking up his own drowsiness
and indifference, and calling himself to a fruitful vigilance. There is
nothing like the deliberate exercise of a power for making it sponta-
neously active. Men who come to have keen and discerning vision
begin by deliberate exercise of the eyes. It is a good and a healthy
thing to stand before a flower and to clearly and strongly challenge
the eyes to attention. It is a profitable thing to stand before some
natural panorama and wake the eyes to diligent quest. Eyes that
are trained in deliberateness come at last to watch instinctively. We
may apply the same reasoning to the realm of the spirit. We must
challenge our own souls, and rouse them to the contemplation of
the things of God. "My soul! look upon this, and look long!" But
let us see to it that when we do incite the attention of our spirits
we give them something worthy to contemplate. "Soul, thou hast
much goods laid up for many years, take thine ease!"[1] That was a
most unworthy spectacle to present to the wondering spirit, and it
would be no surprise if, after a single glance, the soul fell back again
into deeper and more perilous slumber.

---

1 Luke 12:19.

Here in my text the Psalmist calls upon his soul to contemplate the manifold glory of God. Let us gaze at one or two aspects of the inspiring vision.

"He only is *my rock.*" Here is one of the figures in which the Psalmist expresses his conception of the ministry of his God. "My rock!" The figure is literally suggestive of an enclosure of rock, a cave, a hiding-place, There are two or three kindred words used in the Old Testament Scriptures which will, perhaps, unfold to us something of the wealthy content of the speech which the Psalmist employs. All the words are suggestive of encirclement; they describe the state of being surrounded, protected, and secured. Here is one of the kindred words, "Thou hast *beset* me behind and before."[1] How perfectly complete is the suggestion of an all-encircling presence, round about me on every side. The ramparts are built up all about me, and the ring of defense is complete. Perhaps there is no experience in human life which more perfectly develops the thought of the Psalmist than the guardianship offered by a mother to her baby-child when the little one is just learning to walk. The mother literally encircles the child with protection, spreading out her arms into almost a complete ring, so that in whatever way the child may happen to stumble she falls into the waiting ministry of love. Such is the idea of "besetment" which lies in this familiar word "rock."

But let me remind you of another kindred word, *"Bind up* the money in thy hand."[2] You place a coin in the palm of your hand, and your fingers close over it, and the precious metal is strongly secured. It is encircled by a muscular grasp. Let us carry the suggestion into the relationships between ourselves and God. Our Father will secure us as a precious jewel in His own clenched hand. His fingers will wrap round about us, and there shall be no crevice through which the sheltered piece may slip. "None shall pluck you out of My hand!" This, then, is the significance of the word "rock." It is a strong enclosure, an invincible ring, a grand besetment within which we move in restful security.

"He is *my salvation.*"Then He not only shields me, but strengthens me! We are not left by protection in the state of weaklings.

---

1 Psalm 139:5
2 Deuteronomy 14:25.

We are nourished and developed into healthy children. Salvation is a wealthy and comprehensive word. It denotes not merely "first aid," the primary treatment given to those who are bruised and wounded by the wayside; it means, also, "last aid," the bringing of the wounded into strength again. Salvation implies more than convalescence, it denotes health. It is vastly more than redemption from sin; it is redemption from infirmity. It offers no mediocrity; its goal is spiritual prosperity and abundance. This promise of health we have in God. He accepts us in our disease; He pledges His name to confer absolute health. "Having loved His own, He loved them unto the end."[1]

"He is *my defense.*" The Psalmist is multiplying his figures that he may the better bring out the richness of his conception. Defense is suggestive of loftiness, of inaccessibility. It denotes the summit of some stupendous, out-jutting, precipitous crag! It signifies such a place as where the eagle makes its nest, far beyond the prowlings of the marauders, away on the dizzy heights which mischief cannot scale. God is my defense! He lifts me away into the security of inaccessible heights. My safety is in my salvation. Purity is found in the altitudes. I have lately been reading the analysis of the air as it is found by the aeronaut at different levels above our metropolis. The heightening grades revealed heightening degrees of purity, until the last microbe appeared to have been left behind. God lifts us to spiritual heights where our very loftiness of thought and feeling is our best defense. "He hath made us to sit with Him in the Heavenly places."[2] In those lofty spheres the pestilential microbe is harmless. "Neither shall any plague come nigh thy dwelling."[3]

In these three words the Psalmist expresses something of his thought of the all-enveloping and protecting presence of God. He is "my rock," "my salvation," "my defense." What, then, shall be the attitude of the soul towards this God? "My soul, *wait* thou only upon God." "Wait!" Or as the marginal rendering so beautifully gives it, "be thou silent unto God." We are to be in the presence of God with thoughts and feelings which are the opposite to those of

---

1 John 13:1.

2 See Ephesians 2:6.

3 Psalm 91:10.

false haste. The spirit of impatience is to be hushed and subdued. There is to be nothing of passion or of heated distemper. Loud murmurings are to be silenced. Our own clamorous wills are to be checked. The perilous heat is to be cooled. We are to linger before God in composure, in tranquillity. We are to be unruffled. It is the unruffled surface of the pool that receives the reflected beauty of the skies. The reflection is clearest where the life is most calm. How much evidence we have of this in the temper and disposition of the Quakers! They are so frequently, and so long, silent unto God that the very peace of God steeps their spirits, and chastens and refines their manners, gives softness to their speech, and appears to impart leisureliness even to the very activities of their bodies. Would it not be wise for us to copy something of their method, and to linger silently and quietly in the presence of our God? Perhaps we are inclined to talk too much in communion with our God. If silent our spirits might be the more receptive. "One evening," says Frances Ridley Havergal, "after a relapse, I longed so much to be able to pray, but found I was too weak for the least effort of thought, and I only looked up and said, 'Lord Jesus, I am so tired,' and then He brought to my mind 'Rest in the Lord,' and its lovely marginal rendering, 'Be silent to the Lord,' and so I was just silent to Him, and He seemed to overflow me with perfect peace in the sense of His own perfect love."

"My *expectation* is from Him." It is to my mind a very fruitful significance that the word translated "expectation" might also be translated "line" or "cord." "The *line* of scarlet thread." The line of all my hope stretches away to Him, and from Him back to me! The Psalmist declares that however circumstances may vary, the cord of his hope binds him to the Lord. Ever and everywhere there is the outstretched line! I stood a little while ago by the sea. Away over the waters above the horizon, there was the moon shining at the full. Between me and the moon there was a golden line of light stretching across the waters. I walked away down the shore and the line moved with me. Wherever I stood there was the golden cord between me and the lamp of the night. The experience came back to me when I was considering the meaning of the Psalmist's words, "My line is from Him." Whether he was in trouble or in joy, in prosperity or adversity, on whatever part of the varying shoreline he stood, there was the golden track between him and his God. "Thine expectation shall not be cut off"; the line shall never be broken.

"I shall not be moved." Of course not! A man whose conception of God is that of "Rock," "Salvation," and "Defense," and who is "silent unto Him," and is bound to Him by the golden "cord" of hope, cannot be moved. But mark how the Psalmist's confidence has grown by the exercise of contemplation. In the outset of the Psalm his spirit was a little tremulous and uncertain. "I shall not be *greatly* moved." But now the qualifying adverb is gone, the tremulousness has vanished, and he says in unshaken confidence and trust, "I shall not be moved."

Chapter 7

MY STRENGTH AND MY SONG!

*The L*ORD *Jehovah is my strength and my song: He also is become my salvation.*—I*SAIAH* 12:2.

The storm is over. Even the distant rumblings have ceased. The righteous, and yet very tender and pitiful, severity of the Lord has perfected its ministry and has passed away. The alienated heart has been constrained by the sharp instrument of suffering to turn its weary self unto God. And now the sun is shining again, the birds are singing, the desert is blossoming like the rose! There is a new heaven and a new earth! "The Lord Jehovah is my strength and my song: He also is become my salvation."

What does this sweet and joyful singer find in God? "My strength"! "My song"! "My salvation"! How extraordinarily rich and comprehensive! Everything is there! All that a man needs in the battle of life is enshrined in this most wealthy and ancient word. "My strength"; the very power to fight! "My song"; with my God I can fight to music; I can march to the war to the accompaniment of the band; I can be a singing warrior, stepping out to the harmonies of heaven! "My salvation"; with my God I fight to victory, to larger liberty, to ever more glorious possessions. I say everything is here, the strength that makes me a warrior, the song that makes me a happy warrior, the salvation which makes me a happy warrior fighting unto richer freedom. Here truly is a perfect equipment for life's battle, and this equipment is absolutely and entirely found in God.

"The Lord Jehovah is *my strength.*" That is primary and

fundamental. The first thing we need is that our weakness be transformed, and that we become possessed of resource. All other gifts are useless if this initial gift be denied. A box of tools would be impotent without the strong hand to use them. There are many gifted lives that are held in languor and are altogether inefficient because the gifts are not backed by this elementary strength. Phrenology is far from being a science, and much of its teachings savor of quackery, but, amid all its vagaries, one lesson has been emphasized, and I think to great advantage, that, however finely built a man's mind may be, it is like a magnificent engine, idle and productless, unless beneath and behind it there is a fine force of executive strength. Our mental powers are built up, layer upon layer, from the domestic sentiments, through the intellectual senses, to the social and moral and spiritual perceptions, but they are all dependent for their vigor and persistence on a primary strength, without which they are altogether impotent. Here is the organ, which leads the musical services of the church. It is a combination of faculties and functions; let the engine power go wrong, and all the constituents will become idle! The engine provides the power in which all the pipes find their requisite strength. "The Lord is my *strength.*" The Lord imparts unto us that primary strength of character which makes everything in the life work with intensity and decision. We are "strengthened with all might by His Spirit in the inner man."[1]

And the strength is continuous; reserves of power come to us which we cannot exhaust. "As thy day so shall thy strength be,"[2] strength of will, strength of affection, strength of judgment, strength of ideals and of achievement. "The Lord is my strength," strength to *go on*. He gives us the power to tread the dead level, to walk the long lane that seems never to have a turning, to go through those long reaches of life which affords no pleasant surprise, and which depress the spirits in the sameness of a terrible drudgery. "The Lord is my strength'," strength to *go up*. He is to me the power by which I can ascend the Hill Difficulty, and not be afraid. "They shall walk and not faint." "The Lord is my strength," strength to *go down*. I heard a man say the other day concerning his growing physical frailty,

1 Ephesians 3:16.
2 Deuteronomy 33:25.

"It is coming down that tires me!" And in other senses it is coming down that tires a great many of us. It is when we leave the bracing heights, where the wind and the sun have been about us, and when we begin to come down the hill into closer and more sultry spheres, that the heart is apt to grow faint. When a man has reached his height, the height of his fame and popularity, and he begins to go down the hill, it is then he requires exceptional resource. "Though I walk through the valley . . . I will fear no ill, for Thou art with me."[1] "The Lord is my strength," strength to *sit still!* And how difficult is the attainment. Do we not often say to one another in seasons when we are compelled to be quiet, "if only I could do something!" When the child is ill, and the mother has to stand by in comparative impotence, how severe is the test! If she could only do something, if she could only exhaust herself in some effective ministry, if she could only open her own veins and give away her blood! But to do nothing, just to sit still and wait, requires tremendous strength. "The Lord is my strength!" "Our sufficiency is of God."

Let us bring out the music of the pronoun which also brings out the wonder of the promise. "The Lord is *my* strength." Is the conjunction presumptuous, to bring the Almighty in communion with me? I made a little toy water-mill the other day for my little girl, and I used the water from the Welsh hills to work it. And we can let in the river of Water of Life to work the little mill of our life, to make all its powers fruitful and effective. Our God is

> A gracious, willing Guest,
> Where He can find one humble heart
> Wherein to rest.[2]

"The Lord is *my song.*" The religious life must not only be characterized by strength but by music. If the life of the Christian is not musical it is because there is not strength enough. Have you ever heard an organ when the wind-power was insufficient? Have you ever listened to a man with defective lung-power try-ing to blow a bugle? The wind with inadequate strength results

---

1 See Psalm 23:4.
2 A quote from *Our Blessed Redeemer, Ere He Breathed* by Harriet Auber.

in imperfect harmonies. It is when the strength is abounding that we have full song. Go to the Book of the Acts, the Pentecostal book, where the Holy Spirit is sweeping men's lives like a mighty wind. Is there any book more full of music and song, with the strain of a triumphant march? Even in the midnight "Paul and Silas prayed and sang praises unto God."[1] It is not otherwise with the Epistles. The power-Epistles are the singing Epistles. In the greatest of the Epistles, when Paul's Spirit-swept soul surveys the wonders of grace, the doxologies are abounding. We can be perfectly sure that if we are melancholic and gloomy we are wrong at the base, we are lacking in resource. Let me return to the illustration I have just used. When I had made the little water-mill, and I turned the tap and let in a little water from the Welsh hill, it ran reluctantly and sluggishly, and without any song. When I still further turned the tap, and let in a stronger supply, the wheel spun round with great speed and hummed in the spinning! That is what we want. More power would make things hum, would make our spirits sing in the riches of grace. How the psalmists sang in the day of their power! How frequently comes the phrase, "I will sing!" And we can depend upon it, it is a singing religion, a religion that sings while it serves, a cheering, musical religion that is going to save the world! Again let us say, "Our sufficiency is of God." "The Lord is *my* song." All my music is from Him. If the Lord fill my soul with power, there shall rise a unique song, a perfectly original strain. Every life will be a new song. Get the elementary strength and "the time of the singing of birds is come."[2]

"The Lord has become *my salvation.*" That is a fine, full-blooded word, literally signifying "wealth of space." It is as though a man had been fighting in a tight corner, and by the aid of immeasurable "strength," used to the accompaniment of a "song," he had fought his way through into a wide space, into larger liberties, into more glorious possessions. Salvation includes deliverance, inheritance, and freedom. This man has fought and sung his way into ever richer inheritances of spiritual liberty. And that may happen to all of us after every one of our battles. The Lord will always become

1 Acts 16:25.
2 Song of Solomon 2:12.

our salvation. And then, surely, after every fresh deliverance the soul will have more strength for its next victory, and in its victory it will sing a larger song, and in its song it will be ready for the next fray! "And they sang a *new* song,"[1] I do not wonder at it, and they changed it every day!

> From victory unto victory
>   His army shall He lead,
> Till every foe is vanquished
>   And Christ is Lord indeed.[2]

---

1 Revelation 5:9.
2 A quote from *Stand Up, Stand Up for Jesus* by George Duffield Jr.

Chapter 8

THE ABIDING COMPANIONSHIP

My Presence shall go with thee, and I will give thee rest.
—Exodus 33:14.

The other morning I went for a walk up the valley of the Tees. My path left the home, passed under the shadow of the County School, crossed the Recreation grounds, wound in and out among the wide-spreading meadows, now and again coming within sight and sound of the swift, eager river, and now veering round and threading the crowded street of the busy market-town, and now narrowing to the little track that led to a new-made grave. And through all the varying way this evangel possessed my mind, "My Presence shall go with thee, and I will give thee rest."

And then suddenly I realized that my walk had been parabolic, and that in all its shifting changes life itself had been portrayed. My walk had been a Pilgrim's Progress, every turning laden with spiritual significance. I had touched life at all its emphases, and the gracious evangel was fitted to all. "My Presence shall go with thee," in the serious affairs of the home, in the serious place of education, in the relaxations of amusement and sport, in the broad, quiet spaces of Nature's strength and beauty, in the stress and speed of business, and along the narrow road that leads to the open grave. The changing road: the unchanging Presence! The shifting environment: "the Friend that sticketh closer than a brother!"[1] "My Presence shall go with thee, and I will give thee rest."

1 Proverbs 18:24.

Whither is our road going to lead? What sudden and unexpected turnings shall we experience? Shall we find the road firm and smooth and easy, or shall we find it rough and "rutty," straining and tiring to the limbs? Will it provide a pleasant saunter, or will it involve bleeding feet? Will it be a green lane, or a stony steep? Will the way be clear and legible as a turnpike, or will it sometimes be faint and doubtful, like an uncertain track across the moor? We do not know: we are alike in a common ignorance: culture and wealth ensure no favor: all distinctions are here wiped out: we are all upon an unknown road, and for everybody the next step is in the mist! "Thou knowest not what a day may bring forth."[1] If it were good for us to know it, we should be taken into the counsels of the Almighty. The knowledge of the future path really matters nothing: the perception of the present companionship matters everything! What of the road? "Thou knowest not now." What then? "My Presence shall go with thee, and I will give thee rest." And so our text entwines the gracious offer of a Companion for the unknown and changing road. It promises the destruction of loneliness, but not the dispersal of the mist. Let me remind you of some of life's lonelinesses which this wonderful Companionship will destroy.

There is the loneliness of unshared sorrow. Is there anything more solitary than sorrow that can find no friendly ear? Sorrow which has an audience can frequently find relief in telling and retelling its own story. How often the bereaved one can find a cordial for the pain in recalling the doings and prowess of the departed! It is a wise ministry in visiting the bereaved to give them abundant opportunity of speaking about the lost. The heart eases itself in such shared remembrance. Grief is saved from freezing, and the genial currents of the soul are kept in motion. But when sorrow has no companionable presence with which to commune, the grief becomes a withering and desolating ministry.

"When I kept silence, my bones waxed old."[2] Aye, there is nothing ages people like the loneliness of unshared grief. And there are multitudes of people who know no friendly human ear into which they can pour the story of their woes. The outlet manward is

---

1 Proverbs 27:1.
2 Psalm 32:3.

denied them. What then? Is the desolation hopeless? *"My* Presence shall go with thee." The story can be whispered into the ear of the Highest. The Companionship is from above. Said one lonely soul, who had been nursing his grief in secrecy, as the stricken dove seeks to hide the arrow that rankles in its breast, "I will pour out my soul unto the LORD," and in the sympathy of that great Companionship his sorrow was lightened, and transfigured, like rain clouds in the sun.

> In the dark and cloudy day,
> When earth's riches flee away,
> And the last hope will not stay,
>   My Saviour, comfort me.
>
> When the secret idol's gone,
> That my poor heart yearned upon,
> Desolate, bereft, alone,
>   My Saviour, comfort me.[1]

There is the loneliness of unshared triumph. I asked a little while ago if there is anything more lonely than sorrow that can find no friendly ear? I am bound to say that I sometimes think that lonely triumph is as desolate as unshared grief. My memory recalls with vivid clearness one of the boys in the school where I received my earliest training. He was an orphan-boy, but more than that, he was perfectly friendless. Those who were nearest to him were all dead, and the entire interest of his guardian exhausted itself in paying the school-fees as they became due. When the holidays came, and we all bounded home, he remained at the school, for he had nowhere else to go. I thought little or nothing about it. Certainly his position did not move me to pain, until one day his loneliness broke upon me with appalling reality, when in the class-lists he appeared as the premier boy in the school. His triumph was most distinguished and brilliant, but he had no one to share it! No father, no mother, no kinsman, no friend! I felt that in his success he was more desolate than in his defeats! His bereavement seemed to culminate in his triumphs!

---

1 A quote from *Saviour Comfort Me* by George Rawson.

Let me illustrate further. I had a friend who in mature life published a book on which he had bestowed the hard labors of many years. Some time before its publication his wife died, and he was left alone. The book received an enthusiastic welcome, and now enjoys high eminence in its own department of learning. I spoke to my friend of his well-deserved reward, and of the triumph of his labors. His face immediately clouded, and he quietly said, "Ah, if only she were here to share it!" I say, his loneliness culminated there, and his sharpest pang was experienced in his sunniest hour.

It is not otherwise with the moral triumphs of the soul. When I sin and falter, I feel I need a companion to whom I can tell the story of my defeat: but when I have some secret triumph I want a companion to share the glow and glory of the conquest, or the glow and glory will fade. Even when we conquer secret sin the heart calls for a Companion in the joy! And here He is! "My Presence shall go with thee!" If you will turn to the book of the Psalms you will find how continually the ringing paeans sound from hearts that are just bursting with the desire to share their joy and triumph with the LORD. They are the communings of victory, the gladsome fellowship of radiant souls and their GOD. His Presence shall go with us, and He will destroy the loneliness of unshared joy.

And there is the loneliness of temptation. Our friends can accompany us so far along the troubled way, and by GOD's good grace they can partially minister to our progress by re-arranging our environment, and removing many of the snares and pitfalls from our path. But in this serious business of temptation it is little that friend can do for friend. The great battle is waged behind a door they cannot enter. The real fight, the death-grip, is not in some public arena, with friends and spectators gathered around; it takes place in awful and desolate loneliness! In the secret place of every temptation no earthly friend can be near. A man might possibly fight with wild beasts, if the theater were a public one, and amid the plaudits of assembled crowds: but to contend with beasts in secret, to slay them behind the closed and muffled door, is desperate and lonely work. But we need not be alone! One Presence can pass the door that leads to the secret place. "My Presence shall go with thee," not as an interested or applauding spectator, but as Fellow-worker,

Fellow-fighter, Redeemer, and Friend. The loneliness of the wilderness is peopled by the ubiquitous presence of the LORD.

And there is the loneliness of death. It is pathetic, deeply pathetic, how we have to stand idly by at the last moment—doctor, nurse, husband, wife, child—all to stand idly by, when the lonely voyager launches forth into the unknown sea! "It is the loneliness of death that is so terrible. If we and those whom we love passed over simultaneously, we should think no more of it than changing our houses" from one place into another. But every voyager goes alone! Alone? Nay, there is a Fellow-voyager! "My Presence shall go with thee." The last, chill loneliness is warmed by the Resurrection Life. There is a winsome light in the valleys, as of the dawning of grander days. "Though I walk through the valley of the shadow of death I will fear no evil, for Thou art with me." "My Presence shall go with thee!" "When thou passest through the waters, I will be with thee, and through the rivers, they shall not overflow thee."

Now, if we only firmly believed this, and clearly realized this gracious Presence, what would be the ministry? Well, we should work without worry. We should step out without dread. We should waste no energy in fruitless fear and sapping care. We should face the unknown *not daunted by our ignorance.* The great Companion may still think it good to deny us the light of comprehension: but then, though we may not comprehend the nature of the entire way, He will see to it that we have light at the next turning of the road. Don't let us be afraid of our ignorance. Our Companion is a great husbander of light, and at the appointed moment, when "His hour is come," He shall "bring forth thy righteousness as the light, and thy judgment as the noonday."[1]

And do not let us be *afraid of our weakness.* You feel about as little like carrying the possible load of the new day as a grasshopper! Never mind! Perhaps that is how we ought to feel. We must leave something for the great Companion to do! Do not let us try to carry our GOD and our burden too! You remember that passage in Isaiah where, with pathetic irony, the prophet declares that the people are busy carrying their gods, when all the time the great Jehovah is waiting to carry the people! No, our little strength will

---

1 Psalm 37:6.

soon leak out. The real combatants are not our weakness versus the
burdens and difficulties of the day, but all these things versus our
Almighty Friend! "My Presence shall go with thee," and thou shalt
lack neither light nor might; "as thy day so shall thy strength be,"
and "at eventide it shall be light."[1]

But we must lean upon Him and allow Him to carry our load.
An aged, weary woman, carrying a heavy basket, got into the train
with me the other day, and when she was seated she still kept the
heavy burden upon her arm! "Lay your burden down, mum," said
the kindly voice of a working man. "Lay your burden down, mum;
the train will carry both it and you." Aye, that's it! "Lay your burden
down!" The Lord will carry both it and you! "I will give thee rest":
not by the absence of warfare, but by the happy assurance of victory: not by the absence of the hill, but by the absence of the spirit
of fainting. "I will give thee rest."

---

1 Zechariah 14:7.

Chapter 9

LIGHT ALL THE WAY

I am the light of the world.—JOHN 8:12.

I AM the light!" breaking up the empire of darkness, making things luminous by the gracious rays of His own presence. "I am the light of the world," breaking upon the tired eyes of men with the soft, quiet glory of the dawn. Twice recently has it been my privilege to watch the sun rise in circumstances of unusual beauty. Long before his appearing we had tokens of his coming. The horizon, and the clouds that gathered in little flocks about the horizon, and banks of clouds further remote abiding motionless in the highest places, began to clothe themselves in appropriate raiment to welcome the sovereign of the morning. Dull greys, gleaming silver, deep reds, dark purple—all available hues were to be seen in that array. Then in the fullness of time the great flame rode out among the encircling glories, making them all appear dim and faint in the presence of his own effulgence.

"I am the light of the world"; and before His coming, His appearance was foretold in tokens of purple and gold. Here and there, in Isaiah and Jeremiah, we have great peaks tipped with the light of the coming day, suggesting the glory in which the whole world would be bathed in after time. "He shall feed His flock like a shepherd";[1] is not that a fore-token of the tenth chapter of John? "Liberty to the captive, and the opening of the prison to them that are bound";[2] is

1 Isaiah 40:11.
2 Isaiah 61:1.

not this the herald of the wonderful happenings which thrill the gospel story through and through? And then, after all these golden hints of promise, there came the Sun, the Sun of Righteousness with healing in His wings, and the whole world passed into a new day.

"I am the light"; and what multitudes of things He illumined! He threw light upon the character of God, upon the nature of man, upon the beauty of holiness, upon the abominableness of sin. He revealed the poverty of the far country, and with a clear, winning light he showed the way back home. The illumination touches everything, enlightening and quickening everywhere. Let me narrow our subject, and bring our consideration into certain immediate aspects and needs of the personal life. Christ is the light and I need Him. When? Where? I need a light in the unknown day of life. I need a light in the unknown night of death. I need a light in the unknown morrow beyond. I want my Lord today, tonight, tomorrow.

I need the light in the unknown day of life. If I interpret myself aright I am in need of three great primary things: I want to see the right way, I want to love it, and I want power to walk in it. The Light of Life will satisfy all these needs and equip me throughout my pilgrimage. How shall we interpret light? Let us begin here. Science tells us of the conversion of forces, how one force can be translated into another, how motion can become heat and heat become light; and this process of translation can be reversed. Our scientific papers have been recently telling us of a great experiment which has been tried in America. A vast machine was invented in the shape of a gigantic windmill, the arms being composed of reflectors catching the light of the sun. The concentrated light, in the form of heat, was then made to generate steam, and the steam was used to drive complicated machinery.

Now in this wonderful invention we have illustrated the process of transformation by which light is converted into heat and heat into motion. In light we have the secret of fire, and in fire we have the secret of movement. So that when my Lord uses the figure of light I may find in its spiritual suggestion satisfaction for all other needs of my life. "I am the light," not only to make lucid but to make fervid, not only to make fervid but to make operative.

The light illumines; the light kindles; the light empowers. The Lord brings to me light that I may know, warmth that I may feel, and power that I may do. He satisfies the mind, He inflames the desire, He communicates energy to the will. In my mind I need the light! "Lord, give me light to do Thy work." When the Saviour of the world takes up His abode in me, illumination is conveyed to two of my powers; the conscience is made to shine with the distinctiveness of a lighthouse, and the judgment glistens with the brightness of a sharp sword. The "eyes of my understanding" are enlightened, and the lamp of the conscience is never suffered to grow dim.

In my desires I need warmth! Bright ideas would not adequately serve my need. If I am cold in desire the lucid ideal will have no allurement. "Lack of desire is the ill of all ills." And when the revelation has been given, aspiration is needed. How often this healthy desire is mentioned in the Word of God! "They desire a better country." "Desire the sincere milk of the Word." "Desire spiritual gifts." Now it is this desire which the Light of the World enkindles. He makes me not only to see the ideal, but to become fervid in spirit. He makes His disciples "burning and shining" lights.

And I need strength in my will! The power to see and the power to feel would not give me perfect equipment. I need the strength to move. In the illustration I employed it was seen how light could be translated into the power of motion; and the Light of Life conveys energy to the spirit which enables it to follow the gleam. In Him we live *and move.* "It is God that worketh in you *to will.*"[1] And so in light and warmth and power the Lord will be to me all that I need in the day of life. I shall know His mind, I shall love His appearing, I shall be strengthened to move at His command.

But the night cometh! *I shall need Him tonight.* Tonight I shall have to lie down and die. Is there any light? "I am the light" He claims that to those who are in Him the night shineth even as the day. What does my Lord do in the hour of death to break up the reign of darkness? He gives us the cheer of sovereignty. "All things are yours . . . death!" Then I do not belong to death? No, death belongs to me. Death is not my master, he is my servant. He is made to minister to me in the hour of translation, and I shall not

1 Philippians 2:13.

be enslaved by his approach. That was a true and beautiful word uttered by Mrs. Booth when she was passing home: "The waters are rising, but I am not sinking!" Death was her minister, floating her forward to glory. "All things are yours . . . death." And my Lord further softens the night by the gracious light of fellowship. "I will be with thee."[1] When we are in fine and congenial company how the time passes! The hours slip away and we marvel when the moment for separation comes. And so it will be in death! Our company will be so rich and welcome that the season will pass before we know it. I think the Christian's first wondering question on the other side will be: "Am I really through? Really?" "Even the night shall be light about thee."[2] It matters not how stormy the night may be, the Light of Life shall never be blown out. "At eventide it shall be light."

And what about the morrow? When the river is crossed, is there any light upon the regions beyond? Am I to gaze into blackness, impenetrable, inscrutable? "I am the light." What kind of light does He give me here? "In my Father's house!" Is there not a softening gleam in the very phrase? Look here for a sheaf of rays of welcome light. "In my Father's house," there is our habitation! "I go to prepare a place for you,"[3] there is the preparation for us! "I will receive you unto myself," there is a welcome for us! Does not this throw the soft light of the morning on the Beyond? The same light which has been given to me along the way of time will shine upon me in the realms of the new day. "The Lord God is the light thereof." So, you see, it is Jesus all the way; my light today, tonight, tomorrow!

> I heard the voice of Jesus say:—
> "I am this dark world's light.
> Look unto Me, thy morn shall rise,
>   And all thy days be bright."
> I looked to Jesus and I found
>   In Him my star, my sun;
> And in that Light of Life I'll walk
>   Till travelling days are done.[4]

---

1 Isaiah 43:2.

2 Psalm 139:11.

3 John 14:3.

4 A quote from *I Heard the Voice of Jesus Say* by Horatius Bonar.

Chapter 10

OUR BRILLIANT MOMENTS

While ye have light believe in the light, that ye may be the children of light.—JOHN 12:36.

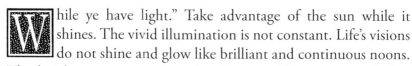hile ye have light." Take advantage of the sun while it shines. The vivid illumination is not constant. Life's visions do not shine and glow like brilliant and continuous noons. The lucid seasons are rare and infrequent. They come and they go, bright intervals in the wastes of grey twilight and darker night. There is an illumination for a moment; in that moment we have a glimpse of reality, and the colors and outlines of things are clearly revealed. "While ye have light believe in the light."

A little while ago, on a dark and stormy night, I wandered along a winding road on a bleak hillside. Things in the distance were hidden from my view, and the things which were near were revealed in weird and portentous guise. Then the clouds divided, and the full moon swept into the rift, and in the blaze of light the road stood out like a white ribbon across the hill, and the whole countryside emerged into view, river and hedgerow and tree. And the rift closed again, the door was shut and again the darkness reigned. But I had taken my bearings, and I could proceed with assured tread. If the enveloping clouds or the mists of the night roll themselves back for a moment, and disclose the stars, by that twinkle of a moment man can adjust and correct his course. Sometimes the illuminant in nature is not the soft light of moon or star. Sometimes the ministry of vision is severe and terrific lightning, bringing hidden things to view with fearful and startling intensity. The flash of a moment can unveil a secret and buried world. "While ye have light believe in the light."

As it is in the realm of nature so it is in the finer region of the soul. We have our brilliant moments. In those moments the near view opens out into the distant prospect and we see things clearly. We are privileged to have "heavenly visions." We have the light! In these bright, lucid seasons we gain some clearer apprehension of God, we look more deeply into the mystery of life, we can behold our ideal possibilities and gaze upon our purified and exalted selves. We see in the winsomeness of duty the repulsiveness of sin, and the charm and fascination of unselfish service. These are the brilliant moments in life, when the clear light is shining upon our changing way. We can never be sure when the revelation may come. We never know when the concealing cloud will divide, and the radiant light will throw her kindly ministry upon our dusky way. We never know just when the veil of the temple will be rent in twain, and our wondering eyes will gaze into the secrets of the holy place.

Sometimes the brilliant moment comes to us when we are contemplating a scene of superlative beauty. Who has not read that wonderful passage in one of Kingsley's letters wherein he describes how the trout stream on Dartmoor, and all its immediate surroundings, opened out into an apocalypse of the unseen? The temporal divided, and he saw God! I heard a man a little while ago describing his experiences amid the unspeakable wonders of the Alps, and his story culminated in a never-to-be-forgotten morning when, away up on the solitary heights, he declared there was "only a film between him and the Lord." I heard another man tell a little company that there had been five or six distinct moments in his life, and perhaps the most commanding of them was a season of sunset in the Austrian Tyrol, when his soul literally trembled in the unfolding glory. Yes, these are brilliant moments, when the heavenly light breaks upon our wondering eyes.

Sometimes the brilliant moment comes in a season of calm and lonely meditation. Everybody else is at rest. The house is quiet. The last book has been put away. And suddenly our surroundings fade away, or are eclipsed, and life's possibilities shine before us in dazzling summits of ambition, pure as Alpine heights. Range upon range of surpassing loveliness breaks upon our spiritual vision, and we behold what we might be in the Lord. It is one of the moments of the Son of Man, a brilliant moment, and we have the light.

Or perhaps the brilliant moment comes to us in the rending ministry of sorrow. It is amazing how far we can see through the tiniest niche and crevice. And when our imprisoning and common-place environment has been shaken and convulsed in some season of upheaval and trouble, through the very rifts of the disaster we often obtain a clear glimpse of a forgotten or neglected world. "In the year that King Uzziah died I saw the Lord."[1] The vision came in a bewildering season of night. Our tears frequently give lucid-ity and range to our views. "Before I was afflicted I went astray, but now . . . !"[2] The light had come in the midnight. The brilliant moment had come in the time of the shadow.

Or perhaps, again, the brilliant moment is experienced in the sanctuary and the ministries of public worship. In some part of the service we gain a wonderful detachment; the ordinary interests that imprison us lose their tyranny; we acquire a spiritual freedom; we soar and see! We gaze upon the Father, we behold our relationship to Him, we feel the greatness of our possible inheritance, and we thrill to the high calling of God in Christ Jesus our Lord. It may be that the detachment and the exaltation spring from a hymn, or from some word from Holy Scripture, or from the leadings of another man's petitions, or from a strain of music. Perhaps it is some face in the congregation that reminds us of another face, and the reminiscence opens the heavens to us. But whatever may be the agent of the illumination, in that momentary vision, however cre-ated, we have a lucid revelation of the reality of things. We see! We have the light!

> Sometimes a light surprises
>   The Christian while he sings.
> It is the Lord, who rises
>   With healing in His wings.[3]

---

1 Isaiah 6:1.

2 Psalm 119:67.

3 A quote from *Sometimes a Light Surprises* by William Cowper.

"While ye have light believe in the light." The brilliant moment passes. The ecstatic revelation comes to an end. The clouds close again. The grey and commonplace twilight returns. How, then, shall we regard and interpret ourselves? Which shall we trust—the revelation of the brilliant moment or the revelation of the familiar twilight? Shall we direct our way according to what we saw at our best, or what we saw in the mediocre season of our life? Here is the answer of our Lord: "Believe in the light." Believe what thou didst behold in thy brilliant moment. Just then, when thy highest powers were at their best, and the season was gracious and genial, take thy bearings. Do not mistrust thy highest, and give thine homage to thy lowest. What didst thou see of thy Lord in thy brilliant moment? What vision didst thou have of His power and His grace and His love? Take that for thy guide: "Believe in the light." What didst thou see of thyself in thy brilliant moment? What of thy present sin, thy possible holiness, thy capabilities of fellowship as a friend and companion of the Lord? "Believe in the light." What didst thou see of duty in thy brilliant moment? Which way did the road take? Over the steep hill or down the seductive vale? Did it reverse thy present purpose and reveal to thee another way? "Believe in the light." What didst thou see of brotherhood in thy brilliant moment? What of pale, beseeching need? What of the helpless and the careworn and the dying? Didst thou see thyself taking a towel and girding thyself? Such, then, is thy possibility, and such is the vision of thy best. "Believe in the light." Do not doubt thy brilliant moments; doubt thy glooms, doubt the revelations of depression, the perverse and crooked creations of despair. The best is always the true. Nothing is too good to be true. It is rather true because it is the good, true because it is the best. "Believe in the light." Let the brilliant vision determine our goings when the ecstatic season is over. Let us act upon what we see at our best. Why? Because the only way to remember a vision is to act it. "Walk in the light lest darkness come upon thee." Aye, that is a terrible truth, and we all know it. How many of our brilliant moments are now things of the night! If we want to keep a brilliant vision we must enact it. Walk in the light of the lucid vision and the vision will endure. "I was not disobedient unto the heavenly vision."[1]

---

1 Acts 26:19.

Let us believe in our best moments, and life as a whole will rise to the plane of best.

And the principle is as applicable to people as to individuals. Let us believe in the revelation of our brilliant moments, in our national possibilities as seen by our nation at its best. Sometimes a man appears upon the grey and commonplace road of low policy and mean expedient and cowardly compromise, and he unfolds a vision of national ideals, and the common life is exalted and glorified. He calls to us, "My fellow men, look upon this," and we turn a reluctant eye, half in derision and half in unbelief. We answer him that his dreamy vision is impracticable. And so we leave the prophet, and we swear by the politician! Oh, the pity of it! "O Jerusalem, thou that stonest the prophets,"[1] the men with the seeing eyes, the men who bring the brilliant moments into the commonplace history of the people! We turn from the prophet because his vision is brilliant. Let us rather "believe in the light." If we will not believe, the prophet passes, the vision fades, and we wander in the confusion of bewildering guesswork instead of looking to the decisive leadership of the light Divine. How often would those leadings have been revealed unto us, "but now they are hidden from our eyes."[2] For individuals and for peoples the brilliant moments are provided in order that we may take our bearings, and by their interpretation adjust the affairs of our ever-changing days.

---

1 See Matthew 23:37.
2 Luke 19:42.

Chapter 11

THE LORD'S GUESTS

Thou preparest a table before me in the presence of mine enemies.
—Psalm 23:5.

This is a desert scene. A hot, panting fugitive is fleeing for his life, pursued and hunted by the forces of a fierce revenge. His crime is placarded on his garments. The marks of blood are upon him. In a moment of passion, or in cool deliberateness, he has maimed and outraged his brother. And now fear has spurred him to flight. Nemesis is upon his track. He takes to the desert! The wild, inhospitable waste stretches before him in shadowless immensity. No bush offers him a secret shelter. No rock offers him a safe defense. He can almost feel the hot breath of his pursuers in the rear. Whither shall he turn? His terrified eyes search the horizon, and in the cloudy distance he discerns the dim outlines of a desert-tent. His excited nerves play like whips about his muscles, and with terrific strain he makes for the promised rest. The way is long! The enemy is near! The air is feverish! The night is falling! The runner is faint! Spurring himself anew, and flinging all his wasting resources into the flight, with the pursuers even at his heels, he stretches out toward the mark, and with one last tremendous exertion he touches the tent-rope and is safe! He is now a guest of the desert-man, and the guest is inviolable. All the hallowed sanctions of hospitality gather about him for his defense. He is taken into the tent, food is placed before him, while his evaded pursuers stand frowningly at the door. The fugitive is at rest. If he can speak at all I think his words will be these, "Thou preparest a table before me in the presence of mine enemies." Such is the undimmed glory of Arab hospitality. To injure a guest is the mark of the deepest depravity. Many of the Bedouins light fires in their encampments to guide the travellers or fugitives to their tents. Many of them keep dogs, not only for the purpose of watching against perils, but in order that, by their bark, they may guide the tired and benighted wayfarer to their place of rest. And so the fugitive finds food and shelter. To touch the tent-rope is to enter the circle of inviolable hospitality. The host is the slave of the guest as long as the guest remains. All the resources of the tent are placed as his disposal. He can lie down in peace, and take his rest in safety. The pursuer is stayed beyond the tent. He can only "look" the revenge he dare not inflict. "Thou preparest a table before me in the presence of mine enemies."

Such is the desert symbol. What is its spiritual significance? The soul is a fugitive, in flight across the plains of time. The soul is pursued by enemies, which disturb its peace, and threaten its destruction. The soul is often terror-stricken. The soul is often a "haunt of fears." There are things it cannot escape, presences it cannot avoid, enemies that dog its track through the long, long day, from morning until night. What are these enemies that chase the soul across the ways of time? Can we name them?

Here is an enemy, *the sin of yesterday*. I cannot get away from it. When I have half-forgotten it, and leave it slumbering in the rear, it is suddenly awake again, and, like a hound, it is baying at my heels. Some days are days of peculiar intensity, and the far-off experience draws near and assumes the vividness of an immediate act. Yesterday pursues today, and threatens it!

> O! I have passed a miserable night,
> So full of ugly sights, of ghastly dreams,
> That, as I am a Christian faithful man,
> I would not spend another such a night,
> Though 'twere to buy a world of happy days,
> So full of dismal terror was the time.[1]

1 A quote from *The Life and Death of Richard the Third* by William Shakespeare.

And what were the "ugly sights" which filled the time with "dismal terror"? They were the threatening presences of old sins, pursuing in full cry across the years! The affrighted experience is all foreshadowed by the Word of God. Whether I turn to the Old Testament or to the New Testament the awful succession is proclaimed as a primary law of the spiritual life. *"Evil pursueth sinners."*[1] That sounds significant of desert-flight and hot pursuit! *"Be sure your sin will find you out!"*[2] as though our sin were an objective reality. The hounds of Nemesis have found the scent, and they are following on in fierce pursuit! "Be sure your sin will find you out." If I turn to the New Testament the dark succession is made equally sure. *"Their works do follow them."*[3] I know these words are spoken of the good, the spiritually-minded, the men and the women who have spent themselves in beneficent sacrifice, "Their works do follow them!" They are attended by the radiant procession of their services, a shining, singing throng, conducting them in jubilation along the ways of time into the temple of the blest! But the converse is equally true. The spiritually-rebellious and unclean are followed by the dark and ugly procession of their own deeds, every deed a menacing foe, reaching out a condemnatory finger, and pursuing them through the portals of death into the very precincts of the judgment-throne. "Their works do follow them." The sin of yesterday is chasing the soul across the plains of today! "Since thou hast not hated blood, even blood shall pursue thee."[4]

Here is another enemy, *the temptation of today*. Yesterday is not the only menacing presence; there is the insidious seducer who stands by the wayside today. Sometimes he approaches me in deceptive deliberateness; sometimes his advance is so stealthy that in a moment I am caught in his snare! At one time he comes near me like a fox; at other times he leaps upon me like a lion out of the thicket. At one time the menace is in my passions, and again it crouches very near my prayers! Now the enemy draws near in the heavy guise of carnality, "the lust of the flesh"; and now in the lighter robe of covetousness, "the lust of the eyes"; and now in the delicate garb of vanity, "the pride of life"! But in all the many guises it is the one foe. In the

1 Proverbs 13:21.
2 Numbers 32:23.
3 Revelation 14:13.
4 Ezekiel 35:6.

manifold suggestions there is one threat. "The enemy that sowed them is the devil."[1] If I am awake I fear! If I move he follows! "When I would do good evil is present with me."[2] "O wretched man that I am, who shall deliver me from the body of this death?"[3] The soul is in the desert, chased by the enemy of ever-present temptation.

Here is a third enemy, *the death that awaits me tomorrow.* "And I looked and beheld a pale horse; and his name that sat on him was Death, and Hell followed with him!"[4] Man seeks to banish that presence from his conscience, but he pathetically fails. The pale horse with his rider walks into our feasts! He forces himself into the wedding-day! "To love and to cherish *until death us do part!*" We have almost agreed to exile his name from our vocabulary. If we are obliged to refer to him we hide the slaughterhouse under rose-trees, we conceal the reality under more pleasing euphemisms. I have become insured. What for? Because tomorrow I may ——. No, I do not speak in that wise. I banish the word at the threshold. I do not mention death or dying. How then? I have become insured, because "if anything should happen to me ——?" In such circumlocution do I seek to evade the rider upon the pale horse. Yet the rider is getting nearer! Tomorrow he will dismount at the door, and his hand will be upon the latch! Shall we fear his pursuit? "The terrors of death compassed me,"[5] cries the Psalmist. "Through fear of death they were all their lifetime subject to bondage,"[6] cries the Apostle of the New Covenant. It is an enemy we have got to meet. "The last enemy . . . is death." Here, then, we are, lone fugitives crossing the desert of time, chased by the sin of yesterday, menaced by the temptation of today, threatened by death tomorrow! The enemies are about us on every side. "My heart is sore pained within me, and the terrors of death are fallen upon me. Fearfulness and trembling are come upon me, and horror hath overwhelmed me."[7] "Oh that I had wings like a dove! for then would I fly away and be

---

1 Matthew 13:39.
2 Romans 7:21.
3 Romans 7:24.
4 Revelation 6:8.
5 Psalm 116:3.
6 Hebrews 2:15.
7 Psalm 55:4, 5.

at rest."[1] Whither can we turn? On the whole vast plain, is there one tabernacle whose tent-ropes we may touch, and in whose circle of hospitality we may find food and refuge and rest?

"God is our refuge and strength, a very present help in time of trouble."[2] In the Lord our God is the fugitive's refuge. "In the secret of His tabernacle shall He hide me."[3] In the Lord our God we are secured against the destructiveness of our yesterdays, the menaces of today, and the darkening fears of the morrow. Our enemies are stayed at the door! We are the Lord's guests, and our sanctuary is inviolable! But what assurance have we that the Lord will take us in? I will give you the assurance. "Hath He not said, and shall He not do it?"[4] I will give you the assurance. The most inspiring way to read the commandments of God is to interpret them also as evangels. Commandments are not only expressive of duties, they are revelations of God. Look into a commandment and you can see what you might be; look into a commandment and you will see what God is. Therefore commandments are not only human ideals, they are expressive of Divine glory. I would know, therefore, what the Lord has commanded, in order that I may look into it for a vision of His face. He has commanded us to be "given to hospitality," to have the camp-fires lit that lost and fear-stricken pilgrims may be guided to shelter and rest! Then, are His camp-fires burning, and is He standing at the tent-door to give the fugitives welcome? I have heard Him apportion the rewards of His kingdom, and these were the terms of the benediction, "I was a stranger, and ye took Me in."[5] Then will the Lord Himself throw back the tent-curtain, and take me out of the fright and darkness into the light and warmth and rest of His own abode!

> If I ask Him to receive me,
>   Will He say me nay?
> Not till earth, and not till heaven
>   Pass away![6]

---

1 Psalm 55:6.
2 Psalm 46:1.
3 Psalm 27:5.
4 Numbers 23:19.
5 Matthew 25:35.
6 A quote from *Art Thou Weary, Art Thou Languid?* by Stephen of Mar Saba.

This, then, is my assurance. What He wants me to do, He does. What He empowers me to be, He is!

> Do I find love so full in my nature, God's ultimate gift,
> That I doubt His own love can compete with it? . . .
> Would I fain in my impotent yearning do all for this man,
> And dare doubt he alone shall not help him, who yet alone can?
>
> ·   ·   ·   ·   ·
>
> Could I wrestle to raise him from sorrow, grow poor to enrich,
> To fill up his life, starve my own out, I would . . .
> Would I suffer for him that I love? So wouldst Thou—so wilt Thou![1]

"I will flee unto Him to hide me."[2]

And what shall I find in the tent? "Thou preparest a table before me in the presence of mine enemies." There is something so exuberantly triumphant in the Psalmist's boast! It is laughingly defiant in its security. The enemies frown at the open door, while he calmly sits down to a feast with his Lord. "Yesterday" glowers, but cannot hurt. "Today" tempts, but cannot entice. "Tomorrow" threatens, but cannot destroy. "O death! where is thy sting?"[3] They are like the enemies which John Bunyan saw just outside the Valley of the Shadow, two giants by whose power and tyranny many had been cruelly put to death, but who can now "do little more than sit in the cave's mouth, grinning at pilgrims as they go by, and biting their nails because they cannot come at them." We taste our joys in the presence of our discomfited foe.

In "the secret of His tabernacle" we shall find a *sure defense*. "Who can separate us from the love of Christ?"[4] We shall find a *refreshing repose*. The shock of panic will be over. The waste of fear will be stayed. We shall "rest in the Lord," and "hide under the shadow of His wing." We shall find an *abundant provision*. Our Host is grandly "given to hospitality." As quaint John Trapp says, "There is not only fullness, but redundance." He giveth "good

---

1 A quote from *Saul* by Robert Browning.
2 Psalm 143:9.
3 1 Corinthians 15:55.
4 Romans 8:35.

measure, pressed down, shaken together, running over!"[1] On the Lord's table there is provision for everybody, and the nutriment is suited to each one's peculiar need.

The only time I have ever heard a sermon on this text was twenty years ago, when I heard Horatius Bonar proclaim its good news to a great company of blind people gathered from the many institutions and homes of the city of Edinburgh. "Thou preparest a table before me," a poor, burdened pilgrim, groping sightless through the ways of time! Aye, there was provision on the table for the blind! And for all of us there is a table prepared and arranged for our need. "In my Father's house there is bread enough and to spare."[2] The desert is cold and weird; in the tent there is warmth and cheer! The desert is the lurking-place of the enemy; in the tent is the glorious fellowship of God! "In the time of trouble He shall hide thee in His pavilion."[3] "Knock, and it shall be opened unto you."[4]

> Rock of Ages, cleft for me,
> Let me hide myself in Thee.[5]

---

1 Luke 6:38.
2 Luke 15:17.
3 Psalm 27:5.
4 Matthew 7:7.
5 A quote from *Rock of Ages, Cleft for Me* by Augustus Toplady.

Chapter 12

HIDDEN MANNA

To him that overcometh will I give to eat of the hidden manna, and will give him a white stone, and in the stone a new name written, which no man knoweth saving he that receiveth it.—REVELATION 2:17.

I think we ought not to refer the fulfilment of this great prophecy to some remote futurity when we have passed through the veil and are in the kingdom of eternal day. If this promise is to be of much worth to me, it must be worth something now. I don't suppose there will ever be a time when I shall need the hidden manna more than I need it now. Certainly there will never come a day when I shall be in greater need of the white stone than I am today. Therefore I want at once to draw this word quite back from that remote day, and regard it as a promise for current need, as a blessing offered to men and women today.

Hidden manna! What is it? Hidden resources; strengthening and sustaining food given to the man who is in the fighting line—a feast upon the battlefield. "Thou preparest a table before me in the presence of mine enemies."

There is nothing that distinguishes one man from another more than staying power. What resources has a man upon which he can draw? What hidden bread can he call out in the dark and impoverished day? You know how that contrast prevails even in the realm of the body; how we contrast and distinguish one from another by the amount he can visibly endure. Why, even of the men who try to achieve the feat of swimming across the Channel the great outstanding contrast is the amount of hidden manna they possess, the amount of secret resources, their capacity to hold out.

Then the contrast prevails in the realm of dispositions. Take the first half-dozen of your friends, and try to measure the length of their tempers; try to put your finger just at the point where irritability begins. You will be amazed how different are the lengths you will have to measure out. One man swiftly exhausts his little store, and has no hidden manna upon which to draw. We say, "his patience was soon spent." Others have hidden manna, and are marvellous in their powers of toleration. How long can you go on, how far can you go in an atmosphere of discouragement, ingratitude, apparent ineffectiveness, and open contempt? How long can you go on teaching a Sunday-school class, and never making a convert? How much hidden manna have you?

The contrast prevails in wider fields still. We hear people saying of a man, "How does he do it?" He is not over strong, sickness is never out of his house, the funeral hearse has often stopped at his door, money does not appear to be plentiful, business is not brisk; his sky is continually overcast. How does he do it? His disposition remains cheery, his hope remains bright, his endeavor abides persistent! What is his staying power? "Hidden manna."

Now, observe, there are two primary emphases of the Christian evangel. The first primary note is that our Lord is acquainted with the secret need of the individual life. "I know My sheep." "Thy Father"—is not this beautiful?—who seeth beneath the skin, who seeth in secret where the kindliest eye of thy dearest friend cannot pierce—"thy Father seeth thy secret need."

The second primary note is this: our God will bring the secret bread to the secret need. Our secret life shall be preserved from starvation, or, to use the words of Paul, our inner life is renewed—fed up, sustained, nourished. That is what constitutes the outstanding contrast between men. Some men are in covenant with the One who has the secret knowledge, and He brings down the hidden manna by which they gain their sustenance and give you and me such keen and frequent surprises. General Booth has not always been the idol of the country. He has rather been the victim of insult, brutality, and open contempt. Where now throughout the length and breadth of the land civic dignitaries hasten to pay him honor, in those very towns and cities in past days he was pelted with the mire of the streets and treated as the very scum of the earth. For thirty or forty years he endured, and no civic or national dignity was conferred upon him, no patronage of the great! Yet he endured—on, on, on! right on to white hairs! What was the secret? "Hidden manna." "I have meat to eat that ye know not of."[1]

What is the second promise of the evangel? "I will give him a white stone." This phrase was running through my brain when I was away for my holiday recently, and in passing along a pebble-strewn beach I picked up a white pebble. I looked at it very intently and inquisitively—and spiritually, in the hope that it would communicate something to me of the significance of the Apostle's figure. It was wonderfully pure; it was intensely hard; it was exceedingly smooth. My Lord will give to me a "white stone." What is the significance of it? My interpretation was this: "I will endow thee with a character pure as a white stone that lies upon the beach, hard and tenacious as that stone, beautifully refined, with all obtrusive and painful angularities smoothed away." Is there anything more exquisitely clean than a white pebble? I don't know how many times the wavelets have washed over the stone until it is cleansed from all defilement. "I will give to thee a life so washed every day by the waters of grace that every part of thy being shall be as clean as a white stone." Perfectly clean is what God purposes us to be. Moral dirt is unnatural. When we are perfectly clean all our powers will work with simplicity and naturalness, as in the very sight of God.

"Perfectly pure I will make thee—and hard!" Oh, not the hardness of insensitiveness, but the hardness of strength. Said one of my young fellows, speaking of another man, "His muscles are as hard as nails." That is the hardness we want in the spirit. Muscular hardness that will not yield to an easy threat or even to a formidable threat, the hardness which is the opposite to flabbiness, softness of limb. The man whose moral muscles are as hard as pebbles, as hard as nails, cannot be broken by any temptations which assail him. That is the character we want—rock-character!

---

1 John 4:32.

Then there is this beautiful addition: "In the stone a new name written." The name I bore in the old life before I turned to the Lord is to be forgotten. A man came to me in my vestry and said, "Do you think God ever forgets and forgives a man's past?" I replied, "God so forgets a man's past that He forgets the man's name! He blots it out, and gives him a new one." We have not to wait for the white stone, but I think we shall have to wait for the unveiling of the new name. No one will enter into the meaning of it except the one to whom it is given. How can any man know my triumphs who has not known my shame? I don't think that Lydia, who lived in Philippi, will ever be able to comprehend the new name of the jailer who lived in the same town. If there had been a kind of Wesleyan fellowship meeting in Philippi, I think their experiences would have been a perfect enigma to each other. I wonder if Billy Bray can ever appreciate the new name given to Henry Drummond, or if Henry Drummond will quite appreciate that of Billy Bray. I wonder if Catherine Booth will understand the new name of Mary Magdalene. I wonder if Mary Magdalene will ever be able to get beneath the surface of the new name of Catherine Booth. We all have our little secrets with our Lord. When He calls you by your name, no one else will respond to it but you.

God will feed us with strength, and endow us with a character like a white stone, and will give to us a unique and individual name. Will you have it? I remember hearing Henry Drummond, addressing a great meeting of graduates and undergraduates, say (and it was about the most sensational thing he ever did say): "Gentlemen, do you mean business? Here is my Lord. If you mean business, give Him your hand—*and stick!*"

Chapter 13

THE REJOICING DESERT

The desert shall rejoice and blossom as the rose.—Isaiah 35:1.

There is nothing more interesting and fascinating than to watch the transformation of the barren into the beautiful. Conversion is often more wonderful than creation. We gaze with extraordinary attention as some half-repellent thing passes through some mysterious process, and in the process becomes lovely. There is always something alluring about the transformation of the desert. In my school days I had a drawing-master who was a very pronounced expert in his profession, and he adorned the walls of the schoolroom with many of his own creations. I have almost completely forgotten those masterpieces, but I perfectly well remember the transformation of one of my own drawings into a thing of comparative beauty. The drawing itself, as I had left it, was fearfully imperfect, and I looked upon it almost with feelings of loathing; but the master touched it and retouched it, and the half-ugly thing became a passable representation of an ancient arch. "The desert was made to rejoice and blossom as the rose." I know two places in Newcastle-on-Tyne, Jesmond Dene and Brandling Park. Jesmond Dene was always beautiful, even before it became a public resort. A few pathways were cut through it, and it was made a little more hospitable to the crowd. But Brandling Park was once an eyesore to the city. It was the place of a common tip, where loads of rubbish were heaped together. And then the municipality determined to change this eyesore into a winsome thing, and they converted it into a beautiful park. Often, on my way to my church, have I rested amid its beautiful green and flowers, and I have rejoiced in the transformation of the repellent into the lovely. "The desert rejoiced and blossomed like the rose." The conversion of Brandling Park was even more wonderful than the original creation of Jesmond Dene.

It is not long since the first trees were planted in the great work of re-afforesting the Black Country. In all broad England there is no stretch of country more depressing than that which lies in dismal waste between Birmingham and Wolverhampton. And now the attempt is being made to transform it, and to redeem the Black Country from its well-deserved notoriety. Yes, it is transformation that arrests our attention. And here is a gracious promise from our God, offering a very miracle of transformation in human life. Just as the eyesore was turned into a park, just as the Black Country is being re-beautified, so the Lord will lay hold of the Black Country of the soul and convert it into His own garden. Let us take the great, mighty promise round about the circuit of our life, let us plant it like an inspiring banner over our deserts, that waving there it may proclaim our wonderful possibilities in the redeeming grace of Christ.

Our Lord will transform *the desert of the soul* and make it blossom as the rose. Who has not known the desert-soul? There is nothing gracious about it, nothing winsome and welcome. When people draw near they can find nothing satisfying in its presence. There is no fruit they can pluck, no water of inspiration they can drink, no grateful shade in which they may find refreshing rest. The whole being is hot and dry and feverish and fruitless. Men speak to one another of such a life and say, "You will get nothing out of him," which means they will not only be denied money, but denied things even more valuable than money; they will be denied time and strength and service. Was not Scrooge in Dickens's "Christmas Carol" a desert-soul? No one drew near to him to pluck a flower or to taste a delicacy or to gather a single green blade. What can be done with a soul like this? Here comes in the uniqueness of the evangel of grace. "The desert shall rejoice and blossom as the rose." Now let us see what can be done.

"I will make the dry land springs of water." First of all, wells

shall break out in the desert-soul. Kindly impulses shall be born. Generous emotions shall flow in plenteous abundance. Gracious feelings shall pervade the once dry and feverish soil. I do not quite know how the Lord will start these springs. He has many ministries, and they are all of them ministers of re-creation. I heard a farmer say a little while ago, "There is nothing like snow for feeding the springs!" And I have known men whose souls have been desert-like, who have been graciously blessed by the Lord under the snows of some chilling sorrow or disappointment. And most assuredly the genial springs have been born again. It is very frequently a seasonable moment, when you want help from anybody, to go after they have passed through some grave and serious affliction. The wells of sympathy are flowing, the first step has been taken in the transformation of the desert.

"*In the wilderness shall waters break out, and streams in the desert.*"[1] The kindly impulse shall become a steady inclination. A spring shall become a river. The emotion shall become a disposition. The soul shall be possessed by genial currents. It may be that the first sign of the gracious conversion will be the flow of tears. Who is there who has not been grateful when some heart, that has been dry and harsh as desert sand, has one day begun to weep? The penitence is the evidence of the wonder-working ministry of the great Restorer, and the life is becoming soft and gracious again.

"*I will plant in the desert the cedar.*"[2] He will not only make the springs to leap and the rivers to flow, He will continue the transformation by the culture of spiritual vegetation. He will plant the cedar, the symbol of strength. The effeminate shall become the masculine, and the soft and yielding shall become the durable and the persistent. There shall be nothing capricious about the life, nothing weak and rootless, but in the transformed desert there shall be virtuous habits with the strength of cedars. "I will set in the desert the fir-tree," the symbol to the Oriental of things sweet and musical. It provided the material out of which they made their harps, and it would suggest to them the end of the desert silence, and the outbreak of praise and song. Well, is not all this a wonderful

1 Isaiah 35:6.
2 See Isaiah 41:19.

transformation of the soul? In the desert of the life there are to come springs and rivers and strong and beautiful trees. And the promise is made to everybody, however dark and terrible may be their need, and however harsh and repellent may be their life. "The desert shall rejoice and blossom as the rose."

Sometimes *our work appears to us like a desert.* One of the great characteristics of the desert is its monotony, and we frequently go to its unchanging wastes for a figure to describe our monotonous toil. In the desert the progress is merely on and on! There is no turn of the road! There is no surprise! And so it is with much of our daily life and calling. There is a great deal of sameness in the work of every man. It is a little round, the well-known track. We trudge it daily, we know every stone in the pavement; and we have become so subdued by the monotony that we have begun to regard ourselves as the victims of drudgery. I think that is how a great many people regard their work. It is a desert and not a garden. I have sometimes spoken to men when they have finished their holiday and returned to their labor, and I have asked them how they have enjoyed it, and they very frequently reply that after such experiences it is very tame returning to the common work.

I stood a little while ago on the Great Orme's Head, on a wonderfully beautiful day, gazing upon the colors of that exquisite coast. There was a fine air blowing over the headland, and everything was fresh and sweet. One who was standing near me suddenly made this remark, "Fancy auctioneering after this!" He had thought of his work, and with the work immediately appeared the desert! His holiday provided the garden, and he was returning to the waste. Now, can the desert of our work be made to blossom like the rose? Most assuredly it can. I wonder how it was with Paul when he was making tents? I feel perfectly sure there was no suggestion of "desert" in the labor. And why did he not regard his work as a desert? Just because there was no desert in his soul. His own soul was a bit of Emmanuel's land, and therefore his work formed a part of the same inheritance. What we are in soul will determine what we see in our work. If our soul is "flat" then everything will drag. The light upon our work comes from our own eyes. If the sunshine is on our souls it will most assuredly beam out of our eyes and rest on our labor.

I knew a cobbler who used to sit at his work just where he could catch a glimpse of the green fields! I think that is suggestive of how we ought to sit at our work. So sit as to catch the glory-light! Let the soul be posed toward the Lord, and the light of His countenance will shine upon it; and the light will beam out of the eyes and our work will appear transfigured. "The desert will rejoice and blossom as the rose."

And surely sometimes *our sorrows* appear as the desert. We pass into experiences that are dark and cold and lonely, and over which there blows a bitter wind. Surely sorrow is a Black Country to untold multitudes of souls! "Can God furnish a table in the wilderness?" Can He feed us in the season of a sorrow? Let us remember it was in the desert that the miracle of the loaves was wrought, and in the desert of our sorrow a harvest miracle may be wrought today. At His word our desert can abound with lilies and violets and heart's-ease and forget-me-nots. "He will also feed thee with the finest of the wheat."[1] Your sorrow shall be turned into joy. Oh, thou troubled soul, turn to the great Wonder Worker, and thy desert shall blossom as the rose!

---

1 Psalm 81:16.

Chapter 14

THE TRANSFORMATION OF THE GRAVEYARD

You did He quicken, when ye were dead through your trespasses and sins.—EPHESIANS 2:1.

D ead through your trespasses and sins," . . . "you did He quicken." The transition is like passing from a graveyard into a sweet meadow in which the children are playing! But this illustration is very imperfect, and in order to make it in any way an adequate analogy of the apostle's thought we must conceive the transformation of the graveyard itself. The graveyard must be converted into a sweet and winsome meadow, and its dead must emerge from their grave clothes in the brightness and buoyancy of little children. It is not a transition from the cemetery to the sweet pastures; it is the transformation of the graveyard itself. "Dead through your trespasses and sins," . . . "you did He quicken"! Or we may change the figure and regard it as the passing of winter into spring. There is winter; cold, bare, flowerless and fruitless. Then there is a feeling of spring in the air. Everything is vitalized and begins to manifest no the signs of growth and increase, and we behold the welcome beauties of the genial season. And here is another winter; "dead through your trespasses and sins." Everything is cold, insensitive, barren. And then comes the vital breath, the vitalizing wind of the Spirit—"you did He quicken." The once dead life begins to manifest evidences of the quickening, and clothes itself with the beauty and glory of the Lord. And "lo, the winter is past, the rain is over and gone, flowers appear on the earth, and the time of the singing of birds is come."[1]

Winter! "Dead through your trespasses and sins." And what are the deadening ministries which create this appalling condition? The apostle mentions two, *"the course of this world"* and *"the prince of the power of the air."*[2] These are the two mighty forces ever at work upon the lives of men, producing paralysis of the higher powers, benumbing and impairing the finer sensitiveness, and sinking all the worthy things in the life to degradation and death.

Here is the first of the deadening ministries, "the course of this world." And is there anything more deadening than the ordinary course and custom of the present world? Look at the world's way of thinking. How deadening is its influence upon the perceptions of the spirit! The thinking of the world always runs on low, planes. It is ever in search of compromise. There is nothing lofty and ideal in its aim and purpose. It seeks purely temporal and transient ends. No man can come under the influence of the world's manner of thought without losing the fine edge of his spiritual powers, and rendering himself insensible to the glorious things of the Spirit. And look at the world's way of speaking. It substitutes gossip for gospel. Its conversation is not seasoned with salt. There is nothing in it to preserve it from corruption. No man can put himself under the influence of the course of the world's speech without reducing his powers of spiritual apprehension. Let a man spend the entire day under the corrupting ministry of worldly speech, and in the evening time he will find that the difficulty of communing with God is incredibly increased. And look at the world's way of doing. The course of this world is always egotistic, emphasizing the interests of self; it is therefore always combative, assuming an attitude of antagonism to one's brother. Now, all these are deadening influences. They work upon the loftier powers of man in sheer destructiveness, and bring his better self to ruin. Men are degraded and sunk into spiritual death by "the course of this world."

And the second of the deadening ministries is "the prince of the power of the air." We are confronted with a personal power, who is ever at work in the realm of evil suggestion and desire. There is a

1 Song of Solomon 2:11, 12.
2 Ephesians 2:2.

great leader in the hierarchy of evil spirits. He is the antagonist of men's welfare, and seeks to destroy the finer faculties by which they hold communion with God. He is *the spirit that now worketh in the sons of disobedience.*[1] When some little flame of carnal desire is kindled in the life, "the prince of the power of the air" blows upon it, and seeks to fan it into fierce and destructive fire. Who has not experienced his influence? It is painfully marvellous how the spark of evil-thinking so speedily becomes a devouring heat! The prince of the power of the air is ever at work blowing upon these incipient fires, in order that in the intense heat of a greater conflagration he may scorch and burn up the furniture of the soul.

Now see how these two deadening ministries work. The apostle declares that they seek to determine our manner of "walk," and also our manner of "life." They seek to subject us to a bondage in which we shall "walk according to the course of this world," and in which we shall "live in the lusts of the flesh, doing the desires of the flesh and of the mind."[2] Now, to influence one's walk is to determine one's conduct; to influence one's life is to determine one's character. By our walk I think the apostle means all the outer movements and activities of the life—what we call our conduct; and by life I think the apostle describes the abiding inclinations and resting-places of the soul—what we call our character. These deadening ministries seek to establish us in the ways of the flesh, to make us choose our dwelling-place in the outer halls and passages of the life, and to neglect the secret and inner rooms where we could hold spiritual communion with God. They lure us into the snare of the bodily senses, and hold us captive there, and so deprive us of that larger life of the spirit which is found in the secret place.

Now, when men's conduct is determined by "the course of this world," and their life is limited by the will of "the prince of the air," all the higher powers in the life languish and droop, and at length pine away in paralysis and death. The deadening ministries complete their work, and man is "dead in trespasses and sins."

Spring! "You did he quicken." It is well to read the earlier verses of this great chapter, and to go slowly through its description of

---

1 Ephesians 2:2.
2 Ephesians 2:3.

the winter time, until we are pulled up by this great and hopeful word: "But God"! The antagonistic word introduces the Lord of the springtime, who is about to break up the bonds and chains of the winter season. And see how graciously the spring is introduced. *"God, who is rich in mercy, for His great love wherewith He loved us, even when we were dead in sins, hath quickened us together with Christ (for by grace are ye saved!)"*[1] Could anything be more gloriously rich in genial and gracious evangel? All the biggest words in the New Testament are introduced in this one verse of Holy Writ. Here we have "grace," and here we have "love," and here we have "mercy," all cooperative in the ministry of breaking up the winter. Grace is the grand, glorious goodwill of God. Love is grace on the march toward us, speeding on a crusade of chivalrous beneficence. Mercy is love arrived, distributing its gifts to those who are enslaved and winter-bound. Surely, here is a rich and all-efficient atmosphere, in which even the firmest tyranny can be melted away! Now watch the ministry of the spring. "Hath quickened us together with Christ." He hath made us alive again. He hath released the appalling grip of the despotic master, and the deadened faculties are alive again.

The quickening is sometimes a painful experience to the one who is being revived. I am told that when a drowning man is brought to shore, and is resuscitated, the renewed flow of life, as the blood-current rushes again through the half-dead and contracted channels, is attended by spasms of agony. And in the life of the spirit I have known the awakening to be a time of keen unrest and pain. But, shall I say, it is only a "growing pain," and is significant of spiritual recreation and expansion? We are acquiring a new sensitiveness toward God and man, and a new capacity, both for joy and pain. *"And hath raised us up together with Him."*[2] We are not only quickened, we are lifted out of our graves. We are taken away from the place where we have been lying, the realm of tyranny where we have been enslaved.

What shall we say then, one to another, when God has lifted us out of the graves? Let us urge one another not to go back to the

1 Ephesians 2:4, 5.
2 See Ephesians 2:6.

cemetery, not even to look upon it, lest we stumble into the grave again. It is a strange and harrowing thing how frequently even saved men will go perilously near to the grave out of which they were redeemed! It is altogether a wise and healthy and secure thing to keep a great space between us and the place of our old enslavement.

"And hath made us sit together with Him in the heavenly places."[1] Said an old Puritan, "A man is where his head is." Of course he is! And as the Christian's head is in heaven, so he is with the Lord in the heavenly places. Here, then, in the coming of the Lord we find our resurrection, "You hath He quickened"; our ascension, "and hath raised us up together"; our enthronement, "and hath made us sit together in the heavenly places with Christ." But in every case our redemption is accomplished *"with Him."* It is all done *"together"!* There is no man so dead that he cannot choose this deliverance by the Lord of life. To choose Him is to have Him; to be willing to have Him is to receive Him. And to receive the Lord is to admit into our life the great Emancipator, who will convert our winter into spring, and turn the life of barrenness into a garden of spiritual fertility and glory.

---

1 Ephesians 2:6.

Chapter 15

COMFORTED IN ORDER TO COMFORT

Blessed be the God and Father of our Lord Jesus Christ, the Father of mercies and God of all comfort; who comforteth us in all our affliction, that we may be able to comfort them that are in any affliction, through the comfort wherewith we ourselves are comforted of God.—2 CORINTHIANS 1:3, 4.

lessed be God!" The apostle begins with his usual doxology. He will have a great deal to say in this epistle about affliction, but he begins upon another note. He begins with the contemplation of the mercies of God, and from that standpoint he surveys the field of his own trouble.

Everything depends upon our point of view. I stood a short time ago in a room which was furnished with wealthy pictures, and I fixed my gaze upon a Highland scene of great strength and glory. The owner of the picture found me gazing at this particular work, and he immediately said, "I am afraid you won't get the light on the hill." And, sure enough, he was right. From my point of view I was contemplating a dark and storm-swept landscape, and I did not get the light on the hill. He moved me to another part of the room, and, standing there, I found that the scene was lit up with wonderful light from above. Yes, everything depends upon our point of view. If you are going to look upon your trouble, the primary question will be, "Where do you stand?" See where the Apostle Paul plants his feet. "Blessed be God!" That is the view-point in the life of faith! Standing there, we shall get the light on the hill. Paul takes his stand on the grace of God, and he gazes upon the ministry of mercies and comfort in the otherwise midnight wastes of affliction and pain. He begins, I say, in doxology. He sings a paean over his mercies and comfort, and lifts his soul in adoration to God.

Now where does the apostle find his comfort? This verse always rears itself before me like a mountain range, in which there is a valley through which there flows a gladdening, refreshing river of mercy and comfort. "Blessed be God!" That is the supreme height. The other end of the text describes the gladdening river of comfort and grace. You see to what elevation he traces his comfort; away up to God! And so his resource is no mere trickle, to be dried up in the day of drought, or swiftly congealed in the nip of the first wintry day. The apostle loved to proclaim the infinitude of his supply, and no wonder, when he found it upon the everlasting hills. It is a very pertinent question which any man can put to himself:—"Will my present comfort last?" It all depends upon where he gets it from. Does he get it from friendships? How grateful is the ministry, and yet is it a dependable supply? Even if our friends are not taken from us by death, can we absolutely depend on the supply of comfort flowing from them to us? Here is a man who had come to the days of drought, and he looked about among his friends, if perchance he might find the waters of sympathy. "I looked on my right hand, and on my left; no man knew me, no one cared for my soul."[1] The river was dry.

Yes, it all depends where we look for our comfort. Do we seek it from books? Again how welcome the service; but it is amazing how the ministry varies. You go to a book one day and the river is full; you return on the morrow and the bed is bleached and dry. We cannot depend on the gracious ministry of our books. Do we seek our comfort in Nature? Again how healing the ministry, and yet how uncertain! I have known a June day deepen a sorrow! I have known a moonlight night throw a heavy soul into a denser gloom! I have known a little flower open out an old wound! We cannot depend upon the comforting ministry of Nature. These are all welcome ministries, gracious ministries, but they are minor ministries, and if we seek our comfort in these, then in the dark and cloudy

---

1 Psalm 142:4.

day we shall be left disconsolate. And so the apostle turns away from the secondary supplies and seeks his resources in the eternal. He hies him away to the infinite and inexhaustible, and his river never fails in the driest and most exacting season. "I will not leave you comfortless." Paul goes away to the heights, and sings his doxology there. "Blessed be God!"

"Blessed be God, *the Father of mercies.*" The Father of pity, of compassion, the Father of that gracious spirit to which we have given the name "Samaritanism." That is the kind of mercy that streams from the hills. Mercy is the very spirit of Samaritanism. It stops by the wounded wayfarer, it dismounts without condescension, it is not moved by the imperative of duty, but constrained by the tender yearnings of humanity and love. It is not the mercy of a stern and awful judge, but the compassion of a tenderly-disposed and wistful friend. Our God is the Father of such mercies. Wherever the spirit of a true Samaritanism is to be found, our God is the Father of it. It was born of Him. It was born on the hills.

It streams from the hills,
It descends to the plain.[1]

Wherever we discover a bit of real Samaritanism we may claim it as one of the tender offsprings of the Spirit of God. With what boldness the apostle plants his Lord's flag on territory that has been unjustly alienated from its owner, and he claims it for its rightful King! "The Father of mercies."

"*The God of all comfort.*" What music there is about the word! It means more than tenderness: it is strength in tenderness, and it is tenderness in strength. It is not a mere palliative, but a curative. It does not merely soothe, it heals. Its ministry is not only consolation but restoration, "Comfort" is "mercy" at work, it is Samaritanism busy with its oil and wine. And again let us mark that whenever we find this busy goodness among the children of men, exercising itself among the broken limbs and broken hearts of the race, the Lord is the fountain of it. He is "the God of all comfort," of every form and kind and aspect. Again I say, how boldly the apostle plants the Lord's flag,

1 A quote from *O Worship the King All Glorious Above* by Robert Grant.

and claims the gracious kingdom of kindly ministries for our God!

"Who comforteth us in all our affliction." Let us note the word in which the apostle describes the condition of the wayfaring pilgrims. They are passing through "affliction"; that is to say, they are in straits, in tight corners. Their way has become narrowed; they are hemmed in by cares or sorrows or temptations, and they are in a tight place. "He comforteth us" in such conditions. The river of mercy and comfort flows our way. Sometimes the comfort comes to us in some secret, mystic ministry which we can never describe. We are feeling very "down," and life has become very tasteless and dreary. We fling ourselves upon our knees, and we expose the dreary waste to the pitying eyes of our God. And suddenly "the desert rejoices and blossoms like the rose!" We cannot give any explanation, but we can exult in the experience.

> It is the Lord who rises
> With healing in His wings.[1]

Sometimes a comfort is mediated to us through the ministry of one of our fellow-men. The apostle never allowed the human messenger to eclipse the Lord who sent him. He had a keen eye for his Lord's comings, even when He wore some lowly human guise. "God comforted me by the coming of Titus!" Happy Paul! to be able to tell by the fragrance of the message that the messenger had come from the King's garden. I would that we might cultivate this fine discernment in order that we might see through the agent to the real doer, and through the ambassador to the King. How often might we be able to say, "God comforted me by the coming of a letter!" "God comforted me by the coming of a kindly service!" "God comforted me by the coming of a friend!" "God comforted me by the coming of . . . ?" Fill up the blank for yourself, and recognize the goodness and mercy of God. "He comforteth us in all our affliction."

"He comforteth us in all our affliction, *that we may be able to comfort them which are in any affliction, through the comfort wherewith we ourselves are comforted of God."* Then the Lord comforts us, not to make us comfortable, but to make us comforters.

1 See Malachi 4:2.

Thou hast received the gift of comfort; now go out and comfort others! "We take God's gifts most completely for ourselves when we realize that He sends them to us for the benefit of other men."

It is not enough for us to have sympathy. Sympathy can be exceedingly fruitless, or it may be exceedingly clumsy, irritating the wound it purposes to heal. There are many men who are exceedingly sympathetic, but they have not the secret ministry of those who have been closeted with the Lord. No, if we would be able to comfort we must ourselves be comforted. They are the expert comforters who have sought and found their comfort in the Lord. They are able to "speak a word in season to him that is weary." They who have been comforted in doubt are the finest ministers to those who are still treading the valley of gloom. They who have been comforted in sickness know just the word which opens the pearly gates and brings to the desolate soul the hosts of the Lord. They who have been comforted in turning from sin and wickedness, and becoming penitent unto God, know just the word to speak to the shrinking Prodigal when he is timidly approaching his father's door.

Let us get away to our God, let us bare our souls to Him, and let us receive His marvellous gifts of comfort and mercy. And then let us use our glorious wealth in enriching other people and by our ministry bring them to the heights.

> O give Thine own sweet rest to me,
>   That I may speak with soothing power
> A word in season as from Thee
>   To weary ones in needful hour.[1]

---

1 A quote from *A Worker's Prayer* by Frances Ridley Havergal.

Chapter 16

THE MINISTRY OF HOPE

Having no hope . . . But now in Christ.—EPHESIANS 2:12, 13.

aving no hope." We are familiar with hopelessness in common life. We know the rout that begins in the sick chamber when hope goes out of the room. So long as the patient remains hopeful the doctor has a mighty helpmeet in his ministry, but when the patient loses heart and hope the doctor strives in the face of almost assured defeat.

The influence is similar in the ministry of the nurse. I was impressed by a phrase uttered in my hearing by a nurse in a conversation which I had with her concerning the nature of her work. "I like a life-and-death case," she said, "with just a chance for life!" She rejoiced in the struggle if the bias was on the side of victory. But when the last chance is gone, and there is no possibility of recovery, and the nurse has to labor confronted by sheer defeat, the service becomes a burdensome task.

It is not otherwise on the battlefield. Armies that go out without the inspiring presence of hope prepare themselves for defeat. I know there is what we call a "courage of despair," but it lacks the very elements of radiant victory. It has dash but no sight; it has force but no song; it is a wild leap and not the jubilant march of strength.

Now, what prevails when hopelessness invades the sick room and the battlefield is also experienced in the more secret life of the spirit, in the realm of religion. When a man becomes hopeless in religious life he loses the very springs of activity, and he sinks in ever-deepening degradation. The Scriptures employ a very power-ful figure to express the state of those in whose life there is no hope. "They that sit in darkness." It is a very graphic picture. Try to realize it. You sit by the fireside on a winter's night, with a bright fire mak-ing the room genial and cheery. You sit on until the fire burns low and eventually dies out, and the warmth gives place to a searching chill. Then the light goes out and darkness is added to the coldness. You sit on. "They that sit in darkness." And there are people whose soul-life is just like that. There is no fire in the grate and their light is gone out, and they abide in cold and dreary desolation, "Having no hope."

Now, what are some of the causes of this dingy and paralyzing hopelessness? Surely I must in the first place mention *the tyranny of sin*. When sin enters into a life and is welcomed there and enter-tained in daily hospitality, certain consequences assuredly happen. One of the first things to happen is this: sin puts out the light of joy. I am persuaded that there is not a man or woman in God's wide world, who persists in deliberate sin, in whose life we could find the light of joy. There is disquiet and unrest, and a sense of a great and hungry uncertainty, and these are incompatible with the abiding presence of joy. No, that light is turned out. But sin goes farther, and proceeds to quench the heat of endeavor. When sin ceases to be a visitor and becomes a tenant in the home of my soul, it assumes the position of master of the house, and I become its servile atten-dant. Repeated experiences of the power of sin create within me a sense of impotence, and I feel how impossible it is to regain my lost sovereignty. My endeavors become more and more lukewarm, my spiritual strivings more and more spasmodic and cold. But sin goes still farther, and eventually scatters and tramples out the very fire of desire. In the earlier stages a man may feel the uselessness of endeav-our while still he may eagerly wish to regain his lost estate, but in the latter stages his very wishes are destroyed and he sinks into the "ill of all ills, the lack of desire."[1] The light of joy has been turned out! The heat of endeavor has been quenched! The fire of desire has died away! And the man is reduced to a state of cheerless and wintry desolation, "Having no hope."

---

1 A quote from *Desire of God* by Frederick William Faber.

The second cause of hopelessness which I will name, is *the tempest of sorrow*. I saw an account, a little while ago, of one of our steamships which had passed through tremendous seas, and the waters had got down into her engine-room and put out the fires. When I read the record I immediately thought of a kindred experience in the spirit, which I find expressed in the ancient words of the Psalmist: "All thy waves and thy billows have gone over me."[1] The passage through heavy seas of sorrow may be attended with complete security, or it may be accompanied by unspeakable loss. It is when the waters of sorrow get down among the fires of the life, the driving passions, the loves and the joys and the hopes, that dire ruin is wrought. It is unfortunately not an infrequent occurrence that the sorrow of a life is permitted to approach the central fires, and the light and warmth and cheer of the life are put out. I have many times heard sorrowing people say, "I feel as cold as stone." May we not say that the engine fire is temporarily out, and that they are drifting in hopeless bewilderment?

And the third of the causes which I will name is *the monotony of labor*. All monotony is tedious and depressing. To be compelled to listen to one persistent note of the organ would be an intolerable affliction, and would weigh the life down in heavy depression. To be obliged to listen even to a monotonous speaker tends to drain away the springs of inspiration. It is the unchanging note that makes the life sink in weariness. And this perhaps is pre-eminently so when one's daily toil is one of unrelieved monotony. There are people whose work calls for no intelligence, no ingenuity, no skill. It makes not the slightest demand upon their thought. It is a purely mechanical service, and works as unsentimentally and as rigidly as a machine. The life looks out every day and sees nothing new. The morning finds it at the old routine. There is no expectancy in the day, no surprise by the road. The hammer of the daily experience hits the same place at every moment, until life settles down into a benumbment which has no vision and no hope. The spring goes out of the spirit, and frequently it happens, as it did in other days, that "Because they have no changes they fear not God."[2]

---

1 Psalm 42:7.
2 Psalm 55:19.

Now, so far we have not brought in the Lord Christ, and just because He has been so deliberately left out, the hopelessness of men has been unrelieved. Let us now bring Him into the dark cold life, and see what happens. "But now in Christ Jesus"—what? What kind of hope does the Master kindle when He enters into communion with a human life? Well, I think He kindles and keeps aflame a threefold hope; hope in the perfectibility of self, hope in the instrumentality of all things, and hope in personal immortality.

Christ kindles hope in the perfectibility of self. He comes to me, a poor sensitive, devil-governed man, and whispers to me that I too can attain to freedom and put on the strength of the ideal man. I stand amazed before the suggestion. Quietly He reassures me and tells me that I too can be perfected. What, I; with the fires out, a poor bit of driftage upon life's sea, that I can be renewed and filled with power and made master of circumstances, and voyage happily and safely to the desired haven? Can I be perfected? I have seen what men can do. I have seen my fellows take a mere refuse place in the city, one of its eyesores, and turn it into a place of beauty. Yes, I have seen the place of refuse transformed into a garden. And even now I hear my fellows speaking confidently of the re-afforesting of the Black Country, and turning the place of slag and cinder heaps, of blackness and death, into a place of sweet growth and pleasantness and beauty. But my Master tells me that the same miracle can be wrought in the realm of the spirit, that the black country in the soul can be re-afforested, that that place of indiscriminate refuse can be turned into the place where the Lord would delight to dwell. "The wilderness shall become a garden, and the desert shall rejoice and blossom as the rose."[1] I, too, can be perfected! This is the hope he kindles, "the hope of glory," "the hope of salvation." The Master begins by breaking the tyranny that holds me captive.

> He breaks the power of cancelled sin,
> He sets the captive free.[2]

And when I have experienced even a little of His emancipating

---

1 See Isaiah 35:1.

2 A quote from *O for a Thousand Tongues to Sing* by Charles Wesley.

ministry my soul walks in a wonderful hope. That is the reason why I am always so anxious that men should have one experience of the power of the Master's grace. One experience will make them the children of a confident hope. Once they have tasted they will want to remain at the feast. "Oh, taste and see how gracious the Lord is." "He will perfect that which concerneth me."[1]

The Master kindles hope in the instrumentality of all things. If He purposes my perfection, then all my circumstances will be made to conspire to the accomplishment of His will. Nothing that comes to me will make me despair. I am hopeful that He will convert everything into a helpmeet and friend. "All things work together for good to them that love God."[2] Even sorrow? Yes, sorrow. Sorrow is one of the "all things," and is subjected to the Master's will, and is one of His instruments for the attainment of His ends. Sorrow can accomplish what comfort would always fail to do. There is a legend that tells of a German baron who, at his castle on the Rhine, stretched wires from tower to tower, that the winds might convert it into an Æolian harp. And the soft breezes played about the castle, but no music was born. But one night there arose a great tempest, and hill and castle were smitten by the fury of mighty winds. The baron went to the threshold to look out upon the terror of the storm, and the Æolian harp was filling the air with strains that rang out even above the clamor of the tempest. It needed the tempest to bring out the music! And have we not known men whose lives have not given out any entrancing music in the day of a calm prosperity, but who, when the tempest drove against them, have astonished their fellows by the power and strength of their music? "Stormy wind fulfilling His word."[3] In Christ I have a hope that everything is made to work for my good. The rough experience is an agent of refinement to polish and take away the rust.

And surely this applies to my work, however monotonous it may be. With the assurance that my Lord will use it for my spiritual profit, into my labor I shall put a song, and the way of drudgery will become the very highway of my Lord. Everything will give me a lift

---

1 Psalm 138:8.

2 Romans 8:28.

3 Psalm 148:8.

if I am in close communion with my Lord.

> Nearer, my God, to Thee,
>   Nearer to Thee;
> E'en though it be a cross
>   That raiseth me;
> Still all my song shall be,
> Nearer, my God, to Thee,
>   Nearer to Thee.[1]

The Master kindles hope in my personal immortality. "Because I live, ye shall live also."[2] "He hath begotten us again unto a living hope."[3] "He that believeth on Me shall never die."[4] What a hope He kindles! Such a hope gives to life an amazing expectancy. When Samuel Rutherford was near his end, he was so gloriously excited at the prospect that those about him had to counsel him to moderate his ecstasy! The fine flavor of that glorious expectancy should pervade all our days. That we are to live for ever with the Lord is a prospect that should fill our life with quiet and fruitful amazement. To have that life in front of us will enable us to set all things in true perspective, and to observe their true proportions. Set "money" in the line and light of immortality, and we at once observe the limits of its ministry and range. Set "rectitude" in the same radiant line, and we see how it clothes itself with abounding glory. Everything must be placed in that long and glorious line or nothing will be truly seen.

These, then, are some of the hopes kindled and inspired by Jesus Christ our Lord. What He kindles He will keep burning. "Having loved His own. He will love them unto the end."[5]

---

1 A quote from *Nearer, My God, to Thee* by Sarah F. Adams.
2 John 14:19.
3 1 Peter 1:3.
4 John 11:26.
5 John 13:1.

Chapter 17

LIFE WITH WINGS

They shall mount up with wings as eagles.—Isaiah 40:31.

"*They shall mount up with wings as eagles.*" Who shall? "They that wait upon the Lord." And waiting upon the Lord is not merely a passing call, but an abiding in Him. Waiting is not so much a transient action as a permanent attitude. It is not the restless vagrant calling at the door for relief, it is rather the intimacy of the babe at the breast.

They who thus wait upon the Lord shall obtain a marvellous addition to their resources. Their life shall be endowed with mysterious but most real equipment. They shall obtain wings. We do well when picturing the angel presences to endow them with wings. At the best it is a clumsy symbolism, but all symbolisms of eternal things are clumsy and ineffective. And what do we mean by wings? We mean that life has gained new powers, extraordinary capacity; the old self has received heavenly addition, endowing it with nimbleness, buoyancy, strength. We used to sing in our childhood, "I want to be an angel." I am afraid the sentiment was often poor and unworthy, and removed our thoughts rather to a world that is to be than to the reality by which we are surrounded today. But it is right to wish to be an angel if by that wish we aspire after angelic powers and seek for angels' wings. It is right to long for their powers of flight, their capacity to soar unto the heights. We may have the angels' wings. Wing-power is not only the reward of those who are redeemed out of time and emancipated from death, and who have entered into the larger life of the unseen glory, but it is the preroga-tive of you and me. "They that wait upon the Lord . . . shall mount up with wings." Waiting upon the Lord will enable us to share the angels' fellowship, to feed on angels' food, and to acquire the angels' power of wing. "They shall mount up with wings as eagles." Now let us see what are some of the characteristics of life with wings.

It is life characterized by buoyancy. We become endowed with power to rise above things! How often we give the counsel one to another, "You should rise above it!" But too often it is idle counsel, because it implies that the friend to whom we give it has the gift of wings; too frequently he is only endowed with feet. If, when we give the counsel, we could give the wings, the things that bind him to the low plains of life might be left behind.

How frequently we are held in bondage by grovelling to the mean and trifling! Some small grievance enters into our life and keeps us from the heights. Some disappointment holds us in depress-ing servitude. Some ingratitude paralyses our service and chills our delight in unselfish toil. Or some discourtesy is done to us, we can-not get away from it. Or, perhaps, it is "the murmur of self-will," or "the storm of passion" which prevents our emancipation. Whatever it may be, and there are a thousand such tyrannies, life is separated from the heavenlies, and becomes utterly mundane, of the earth earthy. Well, now, when we get the wings we have the power to rise above these trifles, and even above the things that may be larger than trifles and may appear like gigantic hills. Wing-power gives buoyancy, and we are enabled to look down even upon the hills and see them beneath our feet. The life with wing-power is not the victim of "the spirit of heaviness." It does not creep along in deep, heavy melancholy. In the day of difficulty and disappointment it can soar and sing at heaven's gate.

Life with wing-power is characterized by loftiness. "They shall mount up!" You know how we speak of the men and women endowed with wings. We speak of a "lofty character," as opposed to one who is low or mean. There are men with low motives, and they move along the low way. There are men with mean affections which do not comprehend a brother. Now, it is the glorious characteristic of the Christian religion that it claims to give loftiness to the life.

There is no feature that the Bible loves more to proclaim than just this feature of "aboveness." It distinguishes the disciples of Christ. See how the ambitions of the book run:—"Seek the things that are above";[1] "Set your mind on things above."[2] It speaks also of dwelling "with Christ in the heavenly places."[3] All this describes the life that looks at everything from lofty standpoints and approaches everything with high ambition. We know these men when they appear. How often one has observed the power of their presence in public meetings! Other speakers have addressed the assembly, and the thought and life of the meeting have grovelled along a mean and questionable way. And then the wing-man comes! He lays hold of the subject, and what happens? Everybody says, "How he lifted it up!" A pure atmosphere came round about the assembly; everybody felt the inrush of a purer air and a finer light. We had mounted up with wings as eagles.

The wing-life is characterized by comprehensiveness. High soaring gives wide seeing. Loftiness gives comprehension. When we live on the low grounds we only possess a narrow outlook. One man offers his opinion on some weighty matter and he is answered by the charge, "That is a very low ground to take." The low ground always means petty vision. Men who do not soar always have small views of things. We require wings for breadth of view. Now see! The higher you get the greater will be the area that comes within your view. We may judge our height by the measure of our outlook. How much do we see? We have not got very high if we only see ourselves; nay, we are in the mire! "Look not every man on his own things, but every man also on the things of others."[4] It is well when we get so high that our vision comprehends our town, better still when it includes the country, better still when it encircles other countries, best of all when it engirdles the world. It is well when we are interested in home missions; better still when home and foreign work are comprehended in our view. We cannot do this without wings, for without the wings we cannot get into the heights. The higher we get

---

1 Colossians 3:1.
2 Colossians 3:2.
3 Ephesians 2:6.
4 Philippians 2:4.

the more we shall see of other parties beside our own. "Lord, we saw one casting out devils in Thy name, and we forbade him, because he followeth not with us."[1] How narrow the outlook! One day the vision of the disciples will be immeasurably enlarged, and that will be when they are dwelling in the heavenly places with Christ. If we remain locked up in an ——ism we shall never see our brethren in the other ——isms. If we rise up into Christ we shall meet our brethren there. Unity is coming by the use of wings! "They shall mount up with wings as eagles."

The wing-life is characterized by proportion. To see things aright we must get away from them. We never see a thing truly until we see it in its relationships. We must see a moment in relation to a week, a week in relation to a year, a year in relation to eternity. Wing-power gives us the gift of soaring, and we see how things are related one to another. An affliction looked at from the lowlands may be stupendous; looked at from the heights it may appear little or nothing. "This light affliction which is but for a moment worketh for us a far more exceeding and eternal weight of glory."[2] What a breadth of view! And here is another. "The sufferings of this present time are not worthy to be compared with the glory which shall be revealed to usward."[3] This is a bird's-eye view. It sees life "whole."

All these are characteristics of the life with wings. And does it not sound a strong and joyful life? "As eagles!" How mighty the bird from which the picture is taken! What strength of wing! And such is to be ours if we wait upon the Lord. We shall be able to soar above the biggest disappointment and to wing our way into the very presence of the sun. "They that wait upon the Lord" shall have all this. Let us abide in waiting and find our joy and our power in the heights.

---

1 Mark 9:38.
2 2 Corinthians 4:17.
3 Romans 8:18.

Chapter 18

THE UNEXPECTED ANSWER

Many were gathered together praying.—ACTS 12:12.

any were gathered together praying." What had prompted the prayer-meeting? "James the brother of John" had been killed "with the sword." "And because Herod saw it pleased the Jews" . . . ! Ah, that is one of the dangerous crises in a man's life! When a man finds that a certain course of conduct is receiving popular applause he is led on to further excesses. He is often doubly betrayed by the seductions of the shouting crowd. A public speaker descends to a coarse and vulgar jest, and because it pleases the baser sort in the audience, and the speaker is awarded a round of applause, he is prone to descend to still further depths of degradation. "He proceeded further to take Peter also"![1] The apostle was arrested, shut up in prison, and guarded by four quaternions of soldiers. And now what can the little company do with whom he has been wont to associate in the evangelical ministry? They have no influence with the king. Not one of the little band has any connections with the imperial house. "Not many noble are called." No material force belongs to them. What, then, is their resource? They can pray. *"Prayer was made without ceasing unto God for him."*

But in such an emergency as this does not a prayer-meeting appear absurd? Here is a man in prison, surrounded by a tenfold defense. The material obstacles are overwhelming. What is the use of a prayer-meeting? Can we pray a man out of his chains, and

---
1 Acts 12:3.

through the prison gate, and through the assembled soldiery? The world regards it as a grotesque expedient. And perhaps there are many Christians who would regard it as legitimate and reasonable to pray for the quietness of Peter's spirit, that he might be kept in boldness of faith and in open communication with his Lord, but who would regard a prayer for his release as trespassing upon forbidden ground. Does not this timidity very frequently spoil the range of our petitions, and rob us of the promised inheritance? If the dominion of prayer is to be limited by the prison gates, we are reduced to a pitiful impoverishment. If the ministry of prayer is absolutely ineffective in the material world, then I, for one, am stupefied. I am told I may pray for mental enlightenment, or for moral strength, or for spiritual perception and gift, but I am warned off the material ground as a domain in which prayer exercises no influence. But I have an initial difficulty. I do not know where the boundary line between the body and the mind is found. In many instances the mental seems to pervade the material, and to control and determine its conditions. If I pray for a brighter mind and obtain it, I gain in addition a healthier body. If I grow in hope I also increase my material resources. If my love is inflamed I am established in the power of endurance. My morals and my digestion are very intimate! And if in this little world, which I call my body, mind and flesh are so intimate, is it not possible that a larger Mind may be intimate with the larger body we call the universe? If my mind can in any way influence and change the ministries of my body, why should not God's mind pervade and control and change the larger ministries of the universe?

And if prayer is the communion of the human mind with the Divine mind, is it altogether incredible that by my fellowship with the Lord I can indirectly exercise the mighty prerogative of influencing the movements even of the material world? And, therefore, I see nothing incredible and illegitimate in praying for favorable weather. It may be that the prayer is sometimes unwise, but the unwisdom of a prayer does not imply the impossibility of the intercourse. I see no need to give our supplications the severe restrictions which many Christians impose. I would rather exercise a glorious liberty, and if Peter is in prison I would pray for the opening of the prison doors, and for the apostle's bodily release.

"And behold, the angel of the Lord came upon him." That was a great moving mission begotten by the ministry of prayer. I will not at the bidding of unbelief reduce the narrative to mere poetry and regard the incident as a commonplace event, for which, if we knew everything, we could find a commonplace explanation. It is one of the profoundest beliefs in my own life that there was a vital connection between the prayer-meeting and the prison. Do not let us throw away our dignities and prerogatives at the cry of the timid, or at the sneer of a flippant unbelief. Do not let us limit our communion. Let us believe that the little prayer-meeting can set in motion ministries which will take the chains from a man's limbs, and lead him out of the iron gates and bring him into healthy freedom.

A little while ago Sir Oliver Lodge met a company of evangelical ministers, and I felt greatly humiliated that we had to receive the warning from his lips not to relinquish the boldness of our rights in the ministry of prayer! This little apostolic prayer-meeting moved about in splendid freedom in their supplication to the Almighty. They prayed for their companion's release, and release was given. "And behold, the angel of the Lord came upon him, and a light shined in the prison: and he smote Peter on the side, and raised him up, saying, Arise up quickly. And his chains fell off from his hands. And the angel said unto him, Gird thyself, and bind on thy sandals. And so he did. And he saith unto him, Cast thy garment about thee, and follow me. And he went out, and followed him: and wist not that it was true which was done by the angel; but thought he saw a vision. When they were past the first and the second ward, they came unto the iron gate that leadeth unto the city; which opened to them of its own accord; and they went out, and passed on through one street; and forthwith the angel departed from him."[1]

Now let us look at these praying people. It is the dead of night. The doors are locked. It is something after the fashion of those prayer-meetings which used to be held in the cellar at Scrooby by the men who founded the commonwealth across the seas. And while one of the little company is praying, a knocking is heard at the door. A damsel named Rhoda goes to the door, and listens to

---

1 Acts 12:7–10.

the voice; she had often heard it, and knew it to be the voice of Peter. Just before she had left the little company, one of the brethren was praying ardently for the apostle's release. Now here he is at the door! *"She opened not the door for gladness."*[1] How strange that is! She was so glad that she became thoughtless! But can gladness confuse the judgment? I know that fear can; fear can throw the powers into panic, and take away the faculty of a calm discretion. And I know that sorrow can lead to mental confusion, and we know not what we do. But here the ministry of bewilderment is joy itself! The incident is simple, and I think most illuminative. Shall we not say that it suggests that we must watch our moments of exultation, our delights, our season of ecstasy? In our joy we may forget many needful things. Is not this true of the joy of a revival? Is it not true that very frequently we open not the gate for gladness? I have known converts who, in the delight of revival meetings, have forgotten common courtesies. They have rapturous eagerness to get away to the foreign field, and they forget to send a letter to their aged mother at home. They ignore the humdrum ministry, in the glad contemplation of the field afar off. There are some people who are so glad in the Lord that they go about writing Scripture-texts on other people's property! Surely that is a forgetfulness which a little vigilance would avoid. I think this is not impertinent teaching. Our joy becomes perilous when it makes us forget the immediate duty. That door! Open it! That little duty! Discharge it! "She opened not the door for gladness."

Now let us go into the meeting itself. Rhoda, I said, had just heard one of the brethren praying, "Lord, restore him unto us!" The damsel eagerly returns with the announcement that Peter is at the gate. Now what? The petition had scarcely fallen from the brother's lips; she had interrupted him in the middle of his petition; and it was probably the suppliant himself who replied to Rhoda, "Thou art mad!" How can Rhoda's announcement be true? Think of the prison, the chains, the soldiers, gate after gate, and especially that notorious iron gate at the last! "Thou art mad!" Again I say, how suggestive the incident! They were praying for an answer; the answer comes to the door; and it strikes them as incredible. I know

---

1 Acts 12:14.

the condition of the little troubled company. There were two empty places in their ranks, and they knew not how soon the vacancies might be multiplied. James was dead and Peter was in prison, and they were bewildered in their distresses. Then they would pray! They prayed for his release, and when his release was given, they received the intimation as the speech of the mad. *"She constantly affirmed that it was so."*[1] And so they went on debating the matter, while all the time the answer was waiting at the door! If it were not too sorrowful the situation would be half-humorous. Surely the best thing would be to open the door at once, which after a while they did. "When they had opened the door they saw him and were astonished."[2]

Now, God's answers to our prayers ought not to surprise us into incredulity. These momentous occurrences ought to be daily commonplaces in our lives. The responses of the Almighty should be grand familiarities. Why should we suppose the herald of the answer to be mad? God is good! God is faithful! It is the most natural of all things that the prison gates should open and the apostle be free. The answer often comes knocking at the door but we don't let it in, and we never know that the answer has been given. We are in an unexpectant mood, and we have never suspected the wealth which the Lord would have left at our gate.

Now let us listen to the word of the apostle. "Go show these things to the brethren."[3] He urges them to be evangelists of the story. Tell these dealings to other people! Go about among the absentees, telling them the wonderful dealings of the Lord. How grand would be the ministry if this were our usual track! Did some gracious answer knock at your door yesterday? Tell it to others. Had you some heartening visitor of grace before the day began? Share it with others. "Come unto me, all ye that fear the Lord, and I will tell you what things He hath done for my soul."[4]

---

1 Acts 12:15.
2 Acts 12:16.
3 Acts 12:17.
4 Psalm 66:16.

Chapter 19

THE CENSER AND THE SACRIFICE

Let my prayer be set forth before Thee as incense; and the lifting up of my hands as the evening sacrifice. Set a watch, O Lord, before my mouth; keep the door of my lips. Incline not my heart to any evil thing, to practice wicked works with men that work iniquity; and let me not eat of their dainties.—PSALM 141:2–4.

et my prayer be set forth before Thee as incense; and the lifting up of my hands as the evening sacrifice. Set a watch, O Lord." How priestly is the entire exercise! Incense! Sacrifice! Supplication! When I had read the verse I rejoiced that I, too, was a priest unto God, and that in Christ Jesus we all have access to the same incomparable privilege and glory. "He hath made us kings and priests unto God."[1] We can all swing the censer; we can all lay the sacrifice upon the altar; we can all engage in the marvellous ministry of intercession.

And then I read the words over again, and I observed the process and order of their thoughts, and I think I can discern in them the primary and all-essential elements in all personal communion with God. These are three in number, and their healthy order is prescribed for us, and it is because we forget or ignore one or two of the three that the fruitfulness of our communion is impoverished. When we draw near to our Lord, all three elements are required of us if our fellowship is to be fruitful, and if we are to return laden with the gifts and glories of the kingdom of grace: first, the incense,

1 Revelation 1:6.

then the sacrifice, and then the intercession.

"Let my prayer be set before Thee as incense." The first thing we have to do when we come into the holy Presence is to swing our censer, and send the odor of our praise upwards to our Lord. The figure is taken from a very popular Eastern custom. Every Oriental is exceedingly partial to sweet odors. He always offers sweet perfume to those whom he delights to honor. In the olden times it was customary in India to scent the roads when the king went out. And what is the significance of the act? It is an acknowledgment of sovereignty, and a tribute of honor and praise. "Let my prayer be set forth as incense"! Let it be "set forth": that is to say, let it begin in adoration and thanksgiving! I think it would be well if sometimes we were to go into the presence of our King just to swing the censer and nothing more. A private praise-service would be an exceedingly efficient and memorable ministry. I remember that Thomas Carlyle, in a letter he wrote to a young friend, offered him this counsel: "Loyal subjects can approach the King's throne who have no requests to make there except that they may continue loyal." I think we may approach the King with just this act of glad obeisance and the pouring forth of the tribute of a grateful heart. We can begin with the incense. It is probable that the worshippers of our day are more inclined to neglect this than our fathers. With what magnificent thanksgivings they preluded their intercessions! Look at the vestibule of this grand hymn-book which ministers to our worship here. Mark the opening section of praise, and see how large is the portion which Dr. Dale has given to the subject of praise. And I think that the proportions of our hymn-book ought to pretty well represent the proportions of our devotion. What sort of vestibule has our private communion? What time do we give to the censer before the suppliant begins? William Law has this very pertinent word in his *Devout Life:* "When you begin your petitions use such various expressions of the attributes of God as may make you most sensible of the greatness and power of the Divine nature." And then William Law gives various examples, which, I am bound to say, would not be helpful to me, as they would imprison my spirit in a coat of mail. But I want to emphasize and commend the principle of it, which is, that our

fellowship should begin with the primary elements of adoration and praise. "Let us come before His Presence with thanksgiving."[1]

I do not think we sufficiently appreciate the effect of praise in the enrichment of our fellowship. The old monasteries used to arrange for relays of monks to be engaged in chanting ceaseless praise, and thereby keeping the entire community susceptible and sweet. The heart is always at its best when it is in the genial influence of praise. There is first of all the preliminary exercise of observing the amazing providences which crowd our ways; for the man who is to praise must become an expert at discernment. It is the man who sees the love-tokens of his Lord crowding about him who comes into His house "in the multitude of His mercies." If we have little or nothing for which to offer praise it is a clear proof that we have been making a most infrequent use of the censer. Let us go into our life, let us ransack its provinces, let us look for the marks of the King's coming and goings, and we shall soon take up the censer. And then when we are in the atmosphere of praise we are one with the spirits of just men made perfect, for it is the atmosphere they breathe in the land of glory. So let us swing the censer:

> Praise, my soul, the King of heaven,
>   To His feet thy tribute bring,
> Ransomed, healed, restored, forgiven,
>   Who, like thee, His praise shall sing?
>   Praise Him, praise Him,
> Praise the everlasting King.[2]

And let *"the lifting up of my hands be as the evening sacrifice."* What is the lifting up of the hands to be like? As a sacrifice. That itself is almost startling. The lifting up of the hands has come to mean an act of supplication, a petition, but here the primary significance is the offering of something to God. It does not betoken a pleading, but a giving, not a request, but a sacrifice. It is like unto the lifting up of the hands of the Roman soldiers when they swore fealty to their emperor and lord. It is our sacramentum.

---

1 Psalm 95:2.

2 A quote from *Praise, My Soul, the King of Heaven* by Henry Lyte.

It is our pledge. It is the yielding of ourselves to the Lord, for whose goodness we have just swung the censer.

Now our sacrifice must never be vague, and therefore meaningless. It is quite easy to sing, "Were the whole realm of nature mine," and to jubilantly proclaim what then would be our sacrifice. The whole realm of nature is not ours, and our responsibility begins and ends with what we have. And therefore we must not lose ourselves in vast professions which have no heart. We must bring the spirit of sacrifice into our present possessions, we must take these things into our hands and lift them up in willing surrender to the Lord. We must hold up our apparent trifles, and let them receive the King's seal. A halfpenny can bear the face and superscription of the king as well as a sovereign. "Let the lifting up of my hands be the sacrifice" of my soul! But even here we must not lose ourselves in a generality. Let us take our powers one by one; our reason, our conscience, our will, and all the manifold spiritual gifts of our God, and let us lay them all upon the altar of sacrifice. "Let the lifting up of my hands be the sacrifice" of my body. And here again, let the surrender be detailed and particular. Let us take our several limbs and members, and brand each one of them with the marks of the Lord Jesus. "Present your body a living sacrifice." And "let the lifting up of my hands be the sacrifice" of my possessions. Let us take the things that bring us comfort and delight and hold them up for the service of the King. There is a tribe in Central Africa which periodically brings its spears and clubs and bows and arrows, and puts them down at the feet of its chief. Then the whole tribe takes again those warlike implements and goes away to fight the battles of their lord. Such must be our way with all our gifts and all our powers. Let us, first of all, swing the incense of our praise, and then take all we are and all we have and lift up our hands in holy sacrifice.

And now, having swung the censer, and sent to heaven the odor of acceptable praise, and having erected the altar and offered to Heaven the sacrifice of our gifts, what remains for us to do? After these primary exercises the Psalmist feels himself justified in proceeding to the gracious ministry of supplication. And see where his petitions begin: "Set a watch, O Lord, before my mouth; keep the door of my lips." I do not wonder he begins there. He asks for the strength of silence. I say, I do not wonder, for he is a persecuted man, and the hardest of all things to a persecuted man is self-restraint. Indeed, it is the severest test of everybody, this controlling of the speech. The Psalmist begins with his cardinal weakness, he goes to the place where he most easily breaks down, he invokes the Divine help at the door of his lips. "By thy words thou shalt be justified, and by thy words thou shalt be condemned."[1] And then he moves from speech to inclination. "Incline not my heart to any evil thing."[2] He goes down among his biases, his leanings, his prejudices, and he prays that he may have an initial bearing toward goodness and virtue and truth. He prays that the elementary bias of his life may be on the side of God. He asks that when many courses are presented to him, he may instinctively lean to the worthiest and the excellent. He beseeches the Lord that he may have the right angle of vision, and that he may survey everything appreciatively from the standpoint of the Almighty. He prays that his dispositions may be pure and true. And lastly his petition moves among his personal pleasures, and he prays for their purification and enrichment. Let me not "practice wicked works with men that work iniquity: *and let me not eat of their dainties."* Aye, that is our peril. When men threaten us we instinctively resist them, but when they offer us dainties we are more easily overcome. If they come to us with a sword we draw our sword in response. But when they come to tickle our palates we easily take the bait. And so the Psalmist prays that these things may never taste dainties at all. If our mouths are perfectly pure, then bitter things will never taste sweet. Our discrimination will be all right if our moral sense is in no wise impaired. And surely our prayer ought to be, "Lord, give me a clean mouth, that the bitter may taste bitter, and the sweet may taste sweet!" We require that refined palate that we may enjoy "the river of God's pleasures." We have got a long way in the Divine life when we appreciate the delicacies of the Lord's table, and find our sweetest things at the King's feast. We are well on the road to holiness when our mouth "is satisfied with good things."

---

1 Matthew 12:37.
2 Psalm 141:4.

Here, then, is the trend of the Psalmist's petitions, beginning with speech, and passing through inclinations to his daily delights. And here is the larger trend of the Psalmist's communion with his Lord, beginning with the gladsome swinging of the censer of praise, and moving through the priestly act of sacrifice to the gracious ministry of supplication.

Chapter 20

THE SCHOOL OF CHRIST

Learn of Me.—MATTHEW 11:29.

his is a word of the Master, to which the heart of man turns with most ready inclination. It is a little favorite rendezvous of pilgrims to Zion. In other parts of the Scriptures we may find only a few footprints or a faintly-outlined road. For instance, there are some parts of Ezekiel, and some parts of what we have foolishly called the Minor Prophets, and large areas of the Book of Revelation, where it is like untrodden moor. But in other places we find a well-made road, suggestive of the passage of multitudinous feet. Such road we find at the twenty-third Psalm, and at the fourteenth of John; and there are many well-trodden parts which are like the immediate circumference of a pool in the meadows where the kine have gathered to drink. And this word of my text marks one of the well-trodden places where thousands of pilgrims are gathered every day.

But just now, amid the abundant wealth of the evangel, I want to concentrate upon one particular part of the counsel, "Learn of Me." How great are the differences which divide us in the mere capacity of learning! Some can suck in knowledge as a sponge takes in water; others throw it aside like the imperviousness of igneous rock. What amazing differences there are in our children in just this quality of receptivity, the power to appropriate knowledge! You give one child a hint and he has got the entire lesson! to other children you have to spell it out slowly, a syllable at a time. And so it is in the realm of religion. There are magnificent scholars in the school of Christ, scholars who can follow hard at the Master's heels, and who can appreciate His lightest word. But there are poorer scholars, like Mr. Ready-to-Halt, who limp on painfully and slowly, and often slip and fall and slide on the upward track. Some of the scholars do not apply themselves, and through sheer indolence they make no progress. Others have no method, and because their study is disorderly they are attended by constant failure. They never seem to rise above the first standard, and they abide in the rudiments of the religious life.

It is to this latter class that I want to try to speak a word of heartening and cheer. A great student and scholar, speaking about quite other roads and realms of knowledge than the purely religious, recently gave some helpful counsel, and I want to lift it from the restricted sphere in which it was employed and apply it to the greater realm of the religious life. "The secret of learning," he said, "is to ask much, to remember much, and to teach much." In what we imperfectly call the secular fields of knowledge these have been found to be fruitful suggestions; I think they will be equally fruitful when applied to our discipleship to Christ. They enfold some of the secrets of successful learning in the school of Christ.

If, then, we would learn of Christ we must "ask much." Now "asking" is a great sign of a fine learner. We cannot come into contact with a man who is finely receptive in any department of knowledge without discovering his fierce inquisitiveness in his own particular realm. I walked out some little time ago with a most learned geologist, and in the course of our journey we passed a common gravel-pit, and at once my friend was all alert and full of inquiry, and immediately began to question the little heap of pebbles which he took in his hand. His "asking" led him to the secrets of a new neighborhood. Within the last few months I walked also in the company of a renowned botanist, and I was amazed at the eager spirit of inquiry which possessed him in every dale and country lane. He was for ever "asking," "seeking," "knocking," and everywhere he found the appointed reward. I am perfectly sure we have got to cultivate this spirit of inquisitiveness in our relation to Christ. We are not great askers in the school. Let us ask for illumination as to character. Let us be full of questioning concerning what the Master calls "heavenly things," the spiritual mysteries, the heavenly glories, the far-off destinies and goals. You will find immense help in such life-quest from the example and experience of the Apostle Paul. A keen asker is a splendid companion to have on a tour. He will put questions which you would never dream of asking; he will talk with the road-mender by the way, and with the old peasant at his cottage door, and with little children on the village green, and the country begins to tell its secrets in answer to the search. Paul, I say, was a splendid asker, and we can train ourselves by the example which is revealed to us in his own great letters. Turn to Colossians, or Ephesians, or Philippians, and mark the things he asks about, and pursue your search along the same lines, and you will most assuredly pass from stage to stage in the Master's school, and have ever-expanding visions of the glory of the Lord.

And let us ask for illumination as to conduct. We not only want knowledge of ideals, but how to apply the ideals to our immediate life. We want principles and we want rules. We want "a light to our path and a lamp unto our feet."[1] We don't ask nearly enough concerning the next step, and the next step, in our forward march. Turn to the Acts of the Apostles and mark the spirit of questioning which always possessed the Apostle Paul in relation to the practice and immediate goings of his life. Or take the simple experiences of Brother Lawrence, and mark how every emergency presents an occasion for making inquiry into God. In this realm we are to be "as little children," voraciously inquisitive, yearning for knowledge of the Divine will, so that we may know the mind of Christ. "Ask much!" We must not be timid in our approach. "He is able to do exceeding abundantly above all that we ask or think."[2] This is one of the great secrets of progressive learning.

"Remember much!" Ah, there is the difficulty for many of us! We can take, but we cannot keep. We can receive an impression, but we cannot retain it. We can do the exposure, but we are not expert in the fixing. We have a vision in the night, but it fades in the glare of the next day. We have a glimpse of glory or of duty, but common

1 Psalm 119:105.
2 Ephesians 3:20.

affairs obliterate it again, and the experience seems to be wasted. This leaky memory is very obtrusive in realms other than religious. How we have to jog our remembrance in the little things of daily life! We knot our handkerchiefs, or we put a ring on another finger, or we call to our aid some system of mnemonics, and all this that we might be able to retain something we have got. Can we call any sanctified expedients to the help of our spirits that we may remember what we have learnt in the school of the Lord? I think we can. We can have, in the first place, some specially appointed time for the ministry of recollection, for reviewing ourselves and our possessions in the presence of the Lord. I place great emphasis upon this expedient. I mean, not so much a time for reading the Scriptures or even for actual supplication, but a season for recalling what we have learned about the Lord, and what we have discovered in the ways of our experience. It is everything to fix definite times for these periods of holy contemplation. Fixity is a great virtue in the discipline of the soul. Fixity helps to engender firm habit, mental bias, and moral inclination. At appointed times the mind is ready for the work, and will more and more answer our bidding to produce its garnered stores. And further, if it be possible, let us have some special place for the ministry, some corner of a room, or some particular street on our way to work, and we shall find that the very place becomes a cooperative friend helping us to revive the partially-effaced impressions. I heard one of the most beautiful spirits in our ministry, one who is now at home in glory, declare some years ago that a particular part of the shoreline of England, where he walked every day in the contemplation of his knowledge of God, had become almost a system of mnemonics. Every headland, and every rock, and every cove silently helped and suggested the findings of past days. You will be amazed at the ministry of places in awaking and confirming the impressions of the soul.

But it will perhaps be best for you to devise your own help-meets for the ministry. You want to recollect God, and the things of God, and the things He has made known to you. Well, sit down and devise some means of "stirring up your remembrance" in this holy exercise. But do not let any one assume that he is alone in the labor of remembrance. We have a great Helper in the sacred work.

"He shall bring to your remembrance whatsoever things I have said unto you."[1] Only let us be honest and eager, sincere and ingenuous, and He will work to the establishment of our souls in the knowledge of God.

"Teach much!" We shall never really know Christ as He is to be known until we begin to tell what we already know. In the realm of religion we never really know until we testify. Until the disciple becomes an apostle he is never an advanced disciple. Every teacher knows this; his knowledge grows while he imparts it. I heard a friend of Watts say in the Tate Gallery some time ago, when he was taking a little party through the famous chamber: "Every time I try to explain these pictures I see more to explain!" In the act of stating a principle the light brightens for ourselves. That, perhaps, is one of the glories of the ministry of Jesus Christ. While we ministers seek to tell about the beauty of the Lord the beauty grows upon our vision. While we declare the grace of redemption, grace more abounds toward us. While we testify as to the way of peace we are led into the more secret place. If we would be fine learners we must be ready teachers. Are you saying you *cannot* be? Is there *anything* you know about the Lord? Tell the little you know, and the little will grow. Have you no sick neighbor, no care-worn friend, no depressed fellow-pilgrim who is fainting on life's way? Teach him the little you know. You will be perfectly amazed at the effect upon your friend, but still more wonderful will be the effect upon yourself. As you go home from that house, the truth which hitherto shone like a candle, will burn like a star. "He that doeth the least of these commandments, and shall teach men so, the same shall be called great."[2] These are some of the secrets of successful discipleship in the school of Christ.

---

1 John 14:26.
2 Matthew 5:19.

Chapter 21

THE MINISTRY OF REST

And He said unto them, Come ye yourselves apart into a desert place, and rest a while: for there were many coming and going, and they had no leisure so much as to eat.—MARK 6:31.

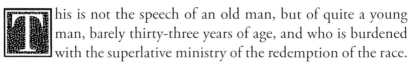his is not the speech of an old man, but of quite a young man, barely thirty-three years of age, and who is burdened with the superlative ministry of the redemption of the race. All the arrangements of His public life are made on the assumption of its brevity. And yet He made time for rest! Sometimes we allow the sacredness of our labor to tempt us to regard rest as indolence and relaxation as waste. True rest is the minister of progress. The hour of seclusion enriches the public service.

What were the special circumstances which impelled our Lord to call His disciples apart? They were twofold. They had just experienced the shock of a great sorrow. John the Baptist had been done to death. The deed had come upon them as an awful collision with their rosiest expectancies. The great Deliverer was near; the Kingdom was at hand; the Divine sovereignty was about to be established; on the morrow He would be on the throne! And yet, here was the pioneer of the kingdom, in the very dawning of the victory, destroyed by the powers of the world. The disciples were stunned and bewildered. The world of their visions and imaginations tottered like a house of dreams. And it was in this season of mental confusion that our Lord called them apart to rest.

But, in the second place, there was the constant distraction of the ubiquitous crowd. *"There were many coming and going."* There is a strangely exciting interest about a multitude. It whips up the life to a most unhealthy speed and tension. And the peril is that we do not realize the intensity when we are in it. When we are on board ship we do not realize how noisy the engines have been until for a moment they cease. We are not conscious of the roar and haste of the traffic of Ludgate Hill until we turn aside into St. Paul's. And it is even so with the influence of a crowd. It acts upon us like an opiate; it externalizes our life, it draws all our interests to the outsides of things, and we are almost unconscious of the distraction. And this was the mesmeric influence in which the disciples were constantly moving. The outsides of things were becoming too obtrusive, and the insides of things were becoming dim. And these same two presences are with us today, the calamity and the crowd, the ministers of bewilderment and distraction. And to us, as to the disciples, the call comes from the Redeemer Himself: "Come ye yourselves apart into a desert place, and rest a while."

Now what will these deliberately contrived seasons of spiritual rest do for the stunned and distracted soul? In the first place, they will help us to realize the reality of the invisible, the immediacy of "things not seen." I know that if we were spiritual experts this fine perception would be experienced everywhere. But the possibility in publicity is conditioned by experiences in private. If we are to have a real sense of God in the crowd it must be by discipline in secret. We require special centers if we would spread the healthy influence over the life. One special day of rest is demanded if the entire week is to become a Sabbath. One special place is to be sanctified if the Lord is to be apprehended everywhere. In my own experience I know that the shocks of the day and the distractions of the crowd tend to remove the Invisible into the dim background, until the Invisible plays no mighty and awe-inspiring part in our lives. It is apart, in the awed quietness and individual loneliness, that the Invisible rears itself like a great mountain. When the pressure of external circumstances is relaxed, and we are alone, the veil of the temple parts asunder, and we are in the holy of holies, and we know ourselves to be in the presence of God. If we practice that Presence in the special moment it will abide with us through the hour.

In the second place, by going apart for rest we shall gain a bird's-eye view of the field of life and duty. In the midst of life's moving affairs we see life fragmentarily and not entire. We note a text, but not a context. We see items, but we are blind to their relationships. We see facts, but we do not mark their far-reaching issue and destiny. We are often ill-informed as to the true size of a thing which looms large in the immediate moment. Things seen within narrow walls assume an appalling bulk. A lion in your back yard is one thing; with a continent to move in it is quite another. There are many feverish and threatening crises which would dwindle into harmless proportions if only we saw them in calm detachment. There are some things which we can never see with true interpretation until we get away from them. There is nothing more hideous and confusing than an oil painting when viewed at the distance of an inch. To see it we must get away from it. Detachment is essential to the comprehension of the whole, and therefore to the discernment of a part. It is not otherwise with life. We are often too much in the thick of things to see them. We cannot see the wood for the trees, the whole for the part, the life for the living. "Come ye apart!" Leave this and that and the other, and from the place of sacred and restful detachment look over the entire field of life and duty, of purpose and destiny, and the fragment shall take its appointed place in the vast design, and shall no longer masquerade as an appalling and overwhelming totality.

Sometimes this season of discerning detachment is forced upon us by the ministry of sickness. The Lord says to a long-time healthy man, "Come apart, I have something to say to thee. I have things to show thee which thou hast forgotten, or which thou hast never seen." And then the man is detached by sickness from the immediate labors to which he has been applying himself with fierce and blinding quest. And what frequently happens, as the outcome of his seclusion, is a transformed conception of life and destiny; "I see things quite differently now!" He had been engrossed in fireworks, and had forgotten the stars. He had been busy building and enlarging his barns and had overlooked his mighty soul. He had been feverish about the transient and negligent of the eternal. "Before I was afflicted I went astray, but now ——!" In the season of seclusion he obtained a corrected vision.

And sometimes a holiday provides the requisite apartness, when life passes in review, and we apprehend its true significance and proportion. I think this is peculiarly true of a minister and his ministry. We are so apt to become riveted to the mere organization, and overlook the very products for which it was devised. We become engrossed with agricultural implements, and we forget the harvest. Now a holiday takes us apart and gives us a more comprehensive view of our work. In some of Dr. Dale's letters, as published in his biography, it is very evident how he utilized his holidays for this most fruitful purpose. He brought all his life under review—his work, the emphasis of his teaching, and the general proportions of his ministry. And what is pertinent for the ministry would be surely fruitful to all men. We may use our holiday times as seasons for looking at things from the standpoint of healthy detachment, and noting the real quality and bearings of our work, its drift, and ultimate destiny.

But what holidays and sicknesses sometimes accomplish we can achieve by more immediate devices of our own choosing. By deliberately retiring from the pressure of our besieging work we can ordain a seclusion-chamber, where we can look at things in the calming, cooling, sanctifying presence of the Lord. In that sacred detachment many obscure things will become clear, "When I thought to know this it was too painful for me; until I went into the sanctuary; then understood I . . ."[1] And in this sacred detachment many previous emphases will be changed. Many a valley shall be exalted, and many a mountain and hill shall be made low. The thing that seemed tremendous shall sink into a plain, and some things, which we had almost ignored, shall rear themselves as the very hills of God.

And there is something further. It is only by this seclusion with the Lord that we can obtain the restoration of our squandered and exhausted strength. Look at this handful of fishermen who were attending our Lord, and mark the life they were leading in these exacting days. They were subjected to the exhausting ministry of constant surprise. We all know how a day of wonders drains our strength, until even wonder itself is spent and weary. These men lived in the thick of the miraculous, and the presentation of every new infirmity was the occasion of a new surprise. I think, I say,

---

1 Psalm 73:16, 17.

wonder itself was dulled, and they became worn and weary. And then, on the top of it all, there was the constant drain of the crowd. The crowd sucks the very energy out of our limbs, and leaves us soft and good-for-nothing. At the time we are in the crowd the drain may be unconscious, but it is none the less real. I know that a multitude provides a stimulus, but the very stimulus consists in opening a sluice-gate of our own precious and secret resource. What a multitude seems to give, it first of all extorts. Here, then, were these men in the midst of all these draining seductions, and they were becoming tired out in body, mind, and soul. "And He said unto them, Come ye apart into a desert place, and rest a while," that in the ministry of seclusion ye may find the means of restoration.

Now this need is as pressing and serious today, perhaps even more so, than in the days of the disciples. Think of the constant drain in modern life. Think of the multiplicity of our correspondence, and every series of letters making its own exaction. Calculate the mere drain upon nerve force, the ceaseless suck upon our most vital resources, and then think of the influence of this constant efflux upon the mind, the organ of discernment, upon the emotions, the ministers of fellowship, and upon the soul, the medium of worship. Our vital strength is oozing out at every pore, and we need means of recuperation.

Now there is nothing that so refreshes the entire man as deep, quiet waiting upon God. Every other refreshment may be welcome, but it is only partial, and will leave some weary power still impaired. Get the soul restored, and every part of the being will feel the mighty influence of its rejuvenation. There are multitudes of men and women who take a weekend at the seaside who would be incomparably more benefited, even in body, if they spent the weekend in quiet, restful communion with their God. There is more real recreation in one hour of communion with Christ than in a whole week of social revelries, however gracious and worthy they may be. "They that wait upon the Lord shall renew their strength; they shall mount up with wings as eagles, they shall run and not be weary, they shall walk and not faint."[1]

---

1 Isaiah 40:31.

Chapter 22

WEALTH THAT NEVER FAILS

The unsearchable riches of Christ.—EPHESIANS 3:8.

"T he unsearchable riches!" The inexplorable wealth, ranging vein beyond vein, mine beyond mine, in land beyond land, in continent beyond continent! "The unsearchable riches of Christ!" And then, side by side with this immeasurable glory, the apostle puts himself. "Unto me, who am less than the least of all saints, is this grace given!"

What an arresting and daring conjunction! "The unsearchable riches" . . . "me, the least of all saints!" It is like some solitary mountaineer contemplating the uplifted splendors of Mont Blanc. "The unsearchable riches" . . . "unto me . . . given!" I turned my eyes away from the printed page, and I saw a bee exploring the wealth of a nasturtium flower. Then I thought of all the flowers in the garden, and of all the flowers in my neighborhood, and of all the flowers in my country, growing in quiet meadows, on heathery moor, and in twilight glen; and then my imagination roamed away to the floral splendors of other lands, bending on the blowing plain or nestling in the hollows of the towering heights, and still further ran my thought to the inconceivable luxuriance of the tropics. And then I came back to my bee, as it visited the hearts of the single flowers in my garden; I thought of that bee setting out to explore the floral wonders of the universe; and then I came back to the apostle, equally busy, extracting juices "sweeter than honey and the honeycomb," and almost bewildered by the vast and overwhelming glories of his inheritance.

"The unsearchable riches of Christ" . . . "unto me" given, "who am less than the least of all saints!" The wealth is inexplorable. It cannot be pegged out. It cannot be finally traced. No inventory can be given. There is always a beyond! His riches are inexhaustible.

> The first-born sons of light
> Desire in vain its depths to see,
> They cannot tell the mystery,
> The length and breadth and height.[1]

Let us turn our contemplation to one or two aspects of this "unsearchable" wealth. The Lord Jesus Christ has created so exacting a conception of Himself in the minds of men that no ministry of man can satisfy it. No human ministry can express it. In all our best representations of the Lord there is always a missing something, an "unsearchable" something, which the most masterly fingers cannot span. Art cannot express Him. I gazed, the other day, upon a powerful picture of our Saviour in conversation with Simon Peter. They were sitting together in Peter's fishing-boat, drawn up upon the beach, and the disciple was busy mending his nets. And as I looked upon the fisherman—strong, muscular, brawny, and watched him as he strayed his fingers, and lifted his keen, restless, impulsive, friendly eyes upon his Master—I said to myself, "That's my Peter! Whenever in coming days I seek communion with him, this is the likeness that will occupy my vision! I want no other! The inspired artist has given me Simon Peter, and I am satisfied!" But when I turned from the fisherman to his Lord my heart gave no leap of contented recognition. No, it was not my Saviour! There were lines of suggestive strength and beauty, but my heart withheld its homage. There was amazing wealth in the representation, but who can express "the unsearchable riches of Christ"? "No, that is not my Saviour," I said, and I turned away unsatisfied.

Nor can literature express Him. The finest lineaments leave the half untold. I suppose that Tennyson has given us his conception of the Christ-man in King Arthur, as Thackeray has given us his in the delicate and lovely likeness of Colonel Newcome, but when

---

1 A quote from *O Love Divine, How Sweet Thou Art* by Charles Wesley.

our hearts have kindled and glowed in their masculine refinements, when we have stood wondering at the mingled strength and transparency of their life as it moves and shines like a glassy sea, our very wonder is chilled if we are told that the likeness must be interpreted as the representation of our Lord. No, a fine man, but not my Saviour! The heart is unsatisfied. And so it is with *all* human ministries, with music and literature and art—they can give us a little of the glory, they can give us diamond wealth as we see it in the jeweller's window, but the diamond mines are unexplored. So exacting is the conception which the Lord Himself has given us, that no human representation is possible, and all our expectations fall dispirited before every attempt to portray "the unsearchable riches of Christ."

But it is not only that our Saviour has created an exacting conception of Himself, He has also, by His "unsearchable riches," created an exacting ideal of human possibility. When His disciples have been emancipated from the bondage of sin, and have been led to occupy some radiant summit in the realm of piety and virtue, even in the midst of their highest attainment they have an overwhelming sense of inexhaustible glories beyond. That was not characteristic of Stoicism. The Stoic got his feet planted upon a lower height, and abode there in undisturbed satisfaction. Most certainly it was not characteristic of the Pharisee. The tragedy of the Pharisee was this— he had finally attained, all his riches were in possession, he had arrived. Pharisaism had a jeweller's window, it had no mines. It spent its time in window-dressing, it never set out on wondering explorations. But the Lord Jesus has created an ideal of character, and has opened out dim and enticing vistas of possibility which leave us, after every conquest, with new dominions yet to be won. Every summit brings a new revelation, the reward of every attainment is a vision of further glory. And so it happens that, altogether unlike Pharisaism, in the ranks of the Lord's disciples the best are the lowliest, those who are furthest up the slopes are the least conscious of their attainments, for they contemplate, with breathless reverence, the far-spreading glories of their "unsearchable riches" in Christ. "Not as though I had already attained, or were already perfect, but I press on . . . !"[1]

---

1 Philippians 3:12, 14.

"Unsearchable riches!" We cannot compute their glory in Christ
our Lord, we cannot put our finger upon their limits in human possibility, and, thirdly, we cannot exhaust their powers of application
to the ever-changing conditions in human life and destiny. In the
Christian life new conditions never find us resourceless. Our wealth
is inexhaustible, and always manifests itself as current coin. An old
well was pointed out to me the other day, of which there are records
stretching back through many centuries. I thought of the strangely
varied and changing life, which had gathered about its birth, and
how it had abundantly satisfied the needs of different environments
that had passed away like dissolving views. Here had come the wan-
dering minstrel, and the devout monk, and the tired soldier, and the
itinerant evangelist, and the farmer and the laborer, and the woman
and the child, and the spring had never failed! Through mediae-
val days, and in the wonderful light of the Renaissance, and in the
fierce, stern days of martial enterprise, and amid the ferment of
the Reformation, and the later kindlings of the evangelical revival,
down to our own day, when nothing harsh or hard seems to disturb
the pastoral peace and simplicity, the well has been flowing, a minister of unceasing refreshment.

It is so with the inexhaustible "riches of Christ," their glory is
found in their immediate applicability to all the changes of our
changing years. They never leave us, we never have to discard them,
they are always up-to-date and pertinent. We can begin to use them
when we are young. It is beautiful, and to me always very wonderful, that our little ones can begin to handle the unsearchable wealth
of Christ. Our "weeniest bairns" paddle in the unsearchable sea, and
if you lift your eyes you may see that same ocean carrying the great
liner upon its broad bosom, and all its unknown freight of sorrow
and joy. And our little ones can put their little feet into the vast sea
of infinite love and grace, and the experience enhances their joy and
liberty. "Suffer little children to come unto Me, and forbid them
not, for of such is the kingdom of heaven."[1] Aye, believe me, our
very youngest have the power to enjoy God. They have a delicate
apprehension, like slender tendrils of climbing plants, by which they
can lay hold of the Eternal, and live the aspiring life of communion

---

1 Matthew 19:14.

with God. And when we grow older, and the apprehension has become a little more matured, larger resources are disclosed to our larger capacity, and the riches are plentiful to the vaster needs. Our Lord never wears out. He is always equal to the problem. He always brims to the new occasion, and in Him we are always full.

> To Thee shall age with snowy hair,
>   And strength and beauty bend the knee:
> And childhood lisp, with reverent air,
>   Its praises and its prayers to Thee.[1]

But it is not only that "the unsearchable riches of Christ" adapt themselves, and reveal their wealth, to the changing condition of our years, it is that in our personal crises, when life suddenly leaps into fierce emergency, their resources are all available, and never leave us in the lurch. There are three great crises in human life—the crisis of sin, the crisis of sorrow, and the crisis of death—and by its ability to cope with these crises every philosophy and every ministry must be finally determined and tried.

How fares it with the riches of Christ in these emergencies? Is the ocean of grace only for childlike paddling, or can it carry a liner? When we come to crises like these, is the Christian's exchequer empty, or is there an abundance of money, and is it current coin? How is it with sin? Are "the unsearchable riches" available? Is there any ministry in broad England dealing with the real virus of sin, and the haunting, paralyzing Nemesis of guilt, except the redeeming grace of Christ? Do you know of any other ministry that is seeking to

> Cleanse the stuffed bosom of that perilous stuff
> Which weighs upon the heart?[2]

Is it not the bare truth to say that every other exchequer is empty? And is it not the bare truth of common experience to say that into the wretchedness of our moral impoverishment, and into the sunless

---

1 A quote from *O Thou to Whom, in Ancient Time* by John Pierpont.
2 A quote from *Macbeth* by William Shakespeare.

places of our spiritual depravity, redeeming grace enters, and begins its mighty work of restoration and enrichment? This was the glory of Christianity to the Apostle Paul, and this it was which inspired his loudest and most triumphant song. "He breaks the power of cancelled sin, He sets the prisoner free!" And Paul found those liberating energies in strange places; they were to him "the treasures of darkness," for they sprang out of the awful poverty and desolations of Calvary. To the Apostle Paul Calvary just meant "the unsearchable riches" of love and grace in conflict with unspeakable powers of guilt and sin, accomplishing their triumphant overthrow, and establishing an open way to the heavenly land of light and peace. "The unsearchable riches" do not "give out" in the high crises of our awful sin and guilt. "What is that you once said?" asked a distressed woman of me the other day in a remote corner of this country, "what is that you once said of the love of Christ to sinners? Tell it me once again!" And she helped my memory until I had recovered the word she wanted, and it was this: "He hath loved thee more than thou hast loved thy sin!" And again I repeat it, that everybody may know, that "where sin abounds, grace doth much more abound,"[1] and that in this deep and dark necessity, where every other form of wealth fails, the "unsearchable riches of Christ" are all-sufficient, for He has "purchased our redemption with His blood."

It is even so with the other crises I have named, the emergency of sorrow and the solemn and austere occasion of death. What wealth of grace He piles up about the sorrow of them that love Him, throwing upon it riches of soft and softening light; until, like the bare screes at gloomy Wastwater when the sunshine falls upon them, colors emerge which make the grief tolerable, as it lies transfigured before the countenance of God. "The people that sat in darkness have seen a great light."[2] "In Thy light shall we see light."[3] "Now are ye light in the Lord."[4]

And at the end of the journey, when we arrive at the tollgate through which we all must pass, we need fear no ill.

---

1 Romans 5:20.
2 Isaiah 9:2.
3 Psalm 36:9.
4 Ephesians 5:8.

The "unsearchable riches" will be still available, and we shall pass quietly and serenely into the realm of clearer air and of larger service. We can never get to the end of "the unsearchable riches of Christ." They are our glory in time: they will be our endless surprise in eternity.

Chapter 23

THE DIVINE ABILITY

Now unto Him that is able to do exceeding abundantly above all that we ask or think, according to the power that worketh in us, unto Him be glory in the Church by Christ Jesus throughout all ages, world without end. Amen.—EPHESIANS 3:20, 21.

How is this doxology born? What are the circumstances which make it spring forth from the apostle's mind and heart? It is preceded by a glorious panorama of spiritual prospect. He has been feasting his eyes upon a vista of bewitching spiritual promise. Let us rehearse the glowing speech in which the vision is described: "That He would grant you, according to the riches of His glory, to be strengthened with might by His Spirit in the inner man; that Christ may dwell in your hearts by faith; that ye, being rooted and grounded in love, may be able to comprehend with all saints what is the breadth, and length, and depth, and height; and to know the love of Christ, which passeth knowledge, that ye might be filled with all the fullness of God."[1] How rich and radiant is the passage! How overwhelming in its visions of glory! But is it all an idle dream? After basking in its splendor for a moment, do we inevitably return to the squalor and meagerness of the commonplace? Is it all a mirage, beautiful but not substantial? Is it a dream, lovely but unreal? Is it too good to be true? Can we enter the promised land? Can we be endowed with regal robes, and walk as kings and queens in the glorious country? Is there any power by which we can

1 Ephesians 3:16–19.

grasp the shining dignities? It is in answer to doubting questions of this kind that the apostle sings his doxology: "Now unto Him that is able to do." The doxology is occasioned by the thought of the dynamic which is ours in God. It is an ideal that may be realized. It is a vision that may be actualized. The promised land is a substantial country, and by the marvellous power of the Almighty the poorest child of time may enter into its possession. Now let us look at the details of the apostle's triumphant song.

"Now unto Him that is able to do." There is something so quiet, so easy, so tremendous in the contents of this word "do." It is not the noisy, obtrusive doings of a manufacturer; it is suggestive of an easy creation. Behind this word "do" there hides that other word "poem," and it is to the naturalness and ease which mark the creation of poetry that the term refers. There is nothing of noise and exertion in the making of a poem; it is a quiet birth; it is the emergence of mysterious power. The majority of us can *make* something that we call poetry, but the vital element is absent. We use the appropriate term in the word "make"; it is something manufactured; it is not suggestive of the coming of a flower or the appearance of a sunrise. The making of poetry results in artifice. It is like the making of artificial flowers, and we can see the supporting wire! I am trying to emphasise that behind this word "do" there is a stupendous and tremendous power, as quiet and as mighty as the power which hides in the birth of the morning. "He is able to do."

"Exceeding abundantly." Here Paul coins a word for his own peculiar use. It seems as though at times the Holy Spirit crowded such great and radiant revelations into the apostle's mind and heart that even the rich vocabulary at his disposal was not sufficient to express them. But when ordinary language fails Paul employs his own. There was no superlative at hand which could describe his sense of the overwhelming ability of God, and so he just constructed a word of his own, the intensity of which can only be suggested in our English phrase "exceeding abundantly." The power flows up, and out, and over! It is a spring, and therefore incalculable. We can measure the resources of a cistern; we can tell its capacity to a trifle. We can register the contents of a reservoir; at any moment we can tell how many gallons it contains. But who can measure the

resources of a spring? It is to this spring-like quality in the Divine power, the exceeding abundance, the immeasurable quantity, that the apostle refers. We can bring our little vessels to the spring and take them away filled to overflowing, and the exceeding abundance remains. The "doing" of our God is an inexhaustible well.

"Above all we ask." The ability of God is beyond our prayers, beyond our largest prayers! I have been thinking of some of the petitions that have entered into my supplications innumerable times. What have I asked for? I have asked my God for forgiveness. I have asked my God for deliverance. I have asked Him for seasons of renewal. Sometimes I have thought that my asking was too presumptuous, it was even beyond the power of God to give. And yet here comes in the apostolic doxology. What I have asked for is as nothing compared to the ability of my God to give. I have asked for a cupful, and the ocean remains! I have asked for a sunbeam, and the sun abides! My best asking falls immeasurably short of my Father's giving. It is beyond all that we can ask.

"Or think." Then His ability is beyond even our imagination! Let us stretch our imaginations to the utmost! Let us seek to realize some of the promised splendors that are ours in Christ. Let our imagination soar amid the offered sublimities of the Word of God. What is it possible for us to become? Think of the splendors of holiness that may be ours! Think of the range of affection that may be ours! Think of the amplitude of service that may be ours! And when our imagination has almost wearied itself in the effort to conceive our possible dignities, let us hear the apostolic song—"Above all that we can think!" I call to mind the men who have been supreme in holy imagination. I think of the marvellous imaginative power of John Bunyan, and his unique capacity for realizing the splendors of the Unseen. But even when I have accompanied John Bunyan, and have been amazed at his power, beyond all his dreams and visions I hear the apostolic word:—"Above all that we can think." I remember Richard Baxter's "Saints' Everlasting Rest." I remember how he deals with the glories of our prospective home, how he seems to have been endowed with special vision for unveiling the raptures of the blessed. But when I have closed Richard Baxter's book in amazed inspiration, I hear the apostolic superlative—"Above all that

we can think." When all our workings and all our thinkings are put together, and piled one upon another, like some stupendous Alpine height, the ability of our God towers above all, reaching away into the mists of the immeasurable.

How does this ability manifest itself toward us? What are the human conditions? *"According to the power that worketh in us."* A certain power on our side creates the possibility in which our God can clothe us with grace and spiritual strength. If our God is to do "exceeding abundantly above all that we can ask or think," there must be a certain power working on our side. There must be a certain energy on the human side, co-operating with the inconceivable strength of the Divine. What is the human power? The power of faith. And what is faith? Faith is a twofold constitution, the elements of which are in vital relation. It is an attitude and a venture. To sever the two is to destroy the life of both. We can no more divide the attitude and the venture and preserve their vitality than we can sustain life by the separation of flesh and blood.

And what *is* the attitude in faith? It is the upward looking of the soul to God. "I will lift up mine eyes unto the hills."[1] "Mine eyes are toward the Lord."[2] The soul looks upward into the face of God that it may discern His mind and hear His voice. And the second element in faith is the element of venture and risk. "I will walk in the paths of Thy commandments."[3] Having heard the Lord's will, risk it! "Thy words were found and I did eat them."[4] When I have discovered the mind of the Lord I must turn His counsel into life. I must incarnate it in conduct. I must take any risk and every risk, and boldly walk in the appointed way. The unity of these two elements constitutes the act of faith. When these are present in the soul, the soul opens out to the wondrous incoming of the Almighty God. When I am willing to risk, God is "able to do." When I surrender, He can impart. The greater my willingness, the richer the river of His grace. If I lose my life I shall find it. "According to your faith be it unto you." "He is able to do . . . according to the power that worketh in us."

1 Psalm 121:1.
2 Psalm 25:15.
3 See Psalm 119:35.
4 Jeremiah 15:16.

It is therefore evident that the act of faith implies the exercise of will. It is more than an emotion; it is an exercise. Before God can "do," my will must be operative. Our wills, however weak, must be on the side of God. "But I have got no will left!" Oh yes, you have! You can will yourself on to your knees. You can will yourself to pray. You can do more than that, you can take the initial steps in obedience. "Rise and walk!" And that was said to an impotent man! But he made the effort to rise, and in making the effort he enabled God "to do"! Use the will you have got. Our God will not carry us as logs. He will cooperate with sincere and endeavoring children. By these conditions we shall become heirs to the wonderful powers that are ours in Christ. There will be no stint in our resources; we shall feel everywhere and feel always that we are more than conquerors through Him that loves us.

Chapter 24

NEW STRENGTH FOR COMMON TASKS

And immediately she arose and ministered unto them.—Luke 4:39.

This woman used her new strength to return to her old duties. She employed her divinely restored health in homely ministries about the house. The first evidence of her restoration was found in her own home. "Immediately she arose and ministered unto them." She did not even make her way to the synagogue to offer public praise to the Lord. Nor did she retire to her chamber, that she might place upon the altar some secret thanksgiving to the King. She just took up her duties with a new strength, and found her joy in immediate ministration to those who were round about her.

It is beautiful to think that one of those to whom she ministered was the Lord Himself. The Lord of all glory sat down to her table, and the once helpless and fever-stricken woman used her new-found strength in ministering to His needs. The mother went on with her motherly work.

Now this is one of the Lord's miracles, but, like all the Lord's miracles, it is full of parabolic suggestion. We read His miracles amiss unless we regard them as vestures of deeper wonders and profounder truths. And I want now to regard this particular act of healing, and the beautiful ministry that followed, as portraying larger workings in which we may all find a share. Here, then, are some of the teachings which I think may be justly inferred from this beautiful story:—

Health is imparted at the touch of the Lord. Our Lord is the
health-center for the race. "In Him was life." It is not that some
life, in certain degree and quality, was found in Him, but that life
of every kind finds in Him its source. "With Thee is the fountain
of life."[1] We cannot find that anywhere else. We can no more find
healthy life apart from the King than we can find heat independent
of the sun. "It pleased God that in Him should all fullness dwell."[2]
Now this Life-source can communicate its treasures to others, and
they are communicated through the ministry of contagion. We come
into touch with our Lord, and by the touch the health-force is conveyed. Let us mark the analogies in the material sphere. Here is the
leper, bearing his loathsome disease, and banned from the society of
his fellows. He draws near to the health-center. "And Jesus touched
him," and by that touch the forces of health routed the regiments of
disease, and the leper became clean as a little child.

It was even so with the blind man. "And Jesus anointed his eyes."
By that wonderful communion the ministry of the Godhead drove
away the impeding scales from the eyes and the man received his
sight. It is the same in the incident before us. Here is the woman
fever-stricken and helpless. "And Jesus touched her," and before the
power of that fellowship the fever left her. Sometimes the initiative
appears to be taken by the children of need. Here is a woman bent
and broken, threading her way through the dense and indifferent
crowd. Now she is borne nearer to the Master, and now carried further away. But at one favorable drift of the crowd she comes near
enough to the Lord to stretch out her hand and touch Him. "Who
touched Me?" The disciples were amazed at the simplicity of the
question, knowing that the multitude was pressing about Him on
every side. But Jesus knew that a touch had been given which had
tapped the fountain! "Virtue hath gone out of Me!" Through the
channels of that communion the woman had received invigoration
which enabled her to stand erect and to walk with ease.

Now this contact comprises a twofold approach, the human and
the Divine. It implies the grasp of two hands, the Healer and the
healed. It necessitates the union of two wills, the man's and his Lord's.

---

1 Psalm 36:9.
2 Colossians 1:19.

Here, again, the material analogies will help our thought. "Lord, if Thou wilt!" There is the projection of the human will, the approach from the side of man. "I will!" And here is the Divine approach, the marvellous condescension of our God. "What wilt thou have Me to do unto thee?"[1] That is the approach of the Lord. "Lord, that I might receive my sight"; that is the approach of the man that is blind. And so, I say, the contact is composed of the unifying of two wills, the will of faith and the will of the redeeming Lord. Our spiritual health begins with the same contact.

> We touch Him in life's throng and press,
> And we are whole again.[2]

No matter what our disease may be, and how deep and established it be, through the power of this union it is driven away. "I will restore health unto thee." When we move our will toward the Lord we may have perfect confidence that He is inclined toward us, and through the mysterious union we become "partakers of the Divine nature."

Health is sustained in the channels of service. When our health has been restored how shall we maintain it? No life can preserve its spiritual health which in any way seeks to be independent of the Lord. Those to whom the Lord imparts health are still dependent upon the Lord. But the health forces will flow to us from our Lord through the channels of service. That is so, I think, in the glory-land, among those who live in the immediate presence of God. Their holiness is maintained in service. "They serve Him day and night."[3] It is not all singing and harping in heaven! And I think that even the harping and the singing will be so arranged as to be ministers to communion. You can depend upon it, we shall need one another there, only it will not be a painful need, and everybody will find their delight and health in serving one another. The "spirits of just men made perfect"[4] are kept in their perfection through mutual ministry.

---

1 Mark 10:51.
2 A quote from *Immortal Love, Forever Full* by John G. Whittier.
3 Revelation 7:15.
4 Hebrews 12:23.

Whether or not this be the principle prevalent in heaven, it is certainly the principle by which health is preserved on earth. "He that would be great among you let him be your minister."[1] And what did Jesus mean by "great"? Certainly He did not suggest the exalted and highly placed. Contacts like these never entered the Master's interpretation of greatness. To be "great" in Jesus' usage of the word is to be morally and spiritually whole. I think, therefore, we may justly transpose His words, and read them in this wise—"He that would be healthy and robust among you let him be your minister." That is how we are to sustain our health; we are to find our strength in service. I think that here we come upon the most conspicuous blot in the character of Christian in the *Pilgrim's Progress.* Everybody is serving him; he is rarely serving anybody. He is not the happiest man, nor does he walk with perfect assurance and triumph. Melancholy often sits upon his shoulders, and he does not walk like a man in exuberant health. I think it is because he is not commonly found in the paths of service. Now Faithful is a healthier man because a more helpful man. He did not see the hobgoblins, nor hear the shrieking spirits that menaced and shouted in the ears of Christian. He was a healthier man, and these things did not come his way. The healthy life is a life of ministration, and the sooner we take to it the better.

"Immediately she arose and ministered unto them." A man once came into my vestry who had just been won from the world, and regenerated by the grace of Christ. I pointed out to him that he must engage in a little service for the King. "Yes," he said, "but I must just feed for a time!" That is a very commonly accepted way, but it is not the appointed way. We get by giving, we feed by feeding. "I have meat to eat that ye know not of." Where had the Master found that food? He had been feeding the poor, fallen woman at the well, and while He fed her soul His own was restored. "When thou art converted, strengthen thy brethren,"[2] and while thou art strengthening thy brother thine own strength shall be preserved. "She arose and ministered unto them."

Our field of service must first be sought in the need that is

---

1 Matthew 20:26.
2 Luke 22:32.

most immediate. Peter's wife's mother began with the humdrum work of the home. Now the first temptation in the converted life is to despise the commonplace. The devil may say to you, now that you are re-born, "You must be a missionary," while all the time the Lord is pointing to a bit of needy work at your own feet. The devil gets your mind set upon Africa, and you ignore your own town; you look for a big sphere, and you ignore your own house. There is nothing more insidious than the temptation to take our eyes away from the immediate need and to wait for an imaginary one. The woman of my text began her ministry in her own house, and that is where we must begin. Is there nothing to sweeten there, to illumine there, to beautify there? We are for ever "seeking for some great thing to do," and there is a bit of duty lying at our feet which needs to be burnished into acceptable brightness.

How is it in your workshop? Is there a Jesus-finish about your work? Is there a Jesus-fragrance about your relationships with your fellow workers? You say you wish to go to the foreign field; suppose your workshop were a bit of India, how are you getting ready for the work? Have you the love-girdle on? Or is the devil saying to you, "You will not want the love-girdle until you are in India"? "Arise and minister." I know a woman who was brought out of darkness into light, and out of bondage into the liberty of the Lord. She lived in one of the poorest courts of our city. And when she was converted she said to herself, "Now I must tidy things up a bit. I must have a Jesus-house, a Martha-and-Mary kind of home. My house must be the tidiest, cleanest, and sweetest house in the court." And such it became. Was not this a bit of real ministry for the King?

We are all so ambitious to be stars, while our Saviour wants us to be street-lamps. And after all, on the muddy, heavy roads at night, and to the trudging, tired wayfarer, the lamp is more useful than the star. "Let your light so shine."[1] We would all like to stand in royal palaces and be cup-bearers to the King, but all the time the King is saying, "Give a cup of cold water in My name!"[2] I am waiting for a great sermon to come my way, and I have waited for years. I want some golden goblet, that I can offer to the critical crowd;

1 Matthew 5:16.
2 Matthew 10:42.

and the Lord is quietly saying to me, "Take a plain cup and give My people to drink!" Some of you young men may be trying to write an eloquent sermon, or some convincing essay on Christian evidences; perhaps, after all, you will serve your Lord better if you will just write home to your mother a little more frequently! Oh, if we would only begin with the intermediate task, and beautify the commonplace road, we should preserve our own spiritual health, and we should bring vigor and grace to others.

Chapter 25

THE MINISTRY OF THE CLOUD

His pavilions round about Him were . . . thick clouds of the skies.
—Psalm 18:11. *The clouds drop down the dew.*—Proverbs 3:20.

His pavilions *are thick clouds!* Then the cloud is not a destructive libertine, some stray, haphazard, lawless force, the grim parent of shadow and chill and tempest! "His pavilions are thick clouds." The clouds are the dwelling-places of God. He lives in them; He moves through them. He pervades them with the gentle ministries of grace and love. "The clouds drop down their dew." Then the clouds are more than shutters; they are springs. They do more than exclude the sunlight; they are the parents of the fertilizing rains and the drenching mists and dews. It is something of a triumph when we have got thus far in our religious faith. In the early days it was believed that only the sunlight was the token and vehicle of our Lord's appearing. But here is a man with a larger and more comprehensive faith. Not only the sunlight, but the cloud also is the minister of His purpose and will. It is not only prosperity which glows with the seal of His favor; adversity also may be a proof of His grace. The cloud may hide the light; it does not destroy it. The cloud does not disprove the light; it is really the proof of the light. Without the warm and genial light there could be no cloud; the cloud is the creation of light. When, therefore, the cloud is forming, it means the sun is working. Raindrops can be traced to sunbeams. Love yearns to send a gentle rain, and so love prepares a cloud. So, the cloud is part of the answer to our prayer for dew.

The sable vehicle carries a brilliant jewel. If, therefore, I have been asking my God for a softening, fertilizing rain, I must not be discomfited by the appearance of a chilling and darkening cloud. If I have been asking for a drenching baptism of dew I must not lose my heart when there comes a confusing mist. I asked for rain; there came a cloud! I asked for dew; there came a mist!

A few years ago, we were asking the Lord to bless our nation; there came a chilling disappointment; the answer was in the cloud! We asked the Lord to save and bless our King; to enrich him with the continual dews of His Holy Spirit; and deep shadows came upon the palace; the answer was in the cloud. We asked the Lord to weld our people together in purer and more fruitful sympathy; and over the people there descended a common sorrow; the answer was in the cloud! We asked the Lord for Coronation blessings! And when all was ready, all was stayed! The pageant halted! Gun and bell and trumpet were silenced! The Coronation ceremonial was checked! a deep gloom ran over the glory. But our answer was in the cloud; the Coronation blessing was more richly given in awakened thought, in more elevated vision, in deepened intercession, in moral increment, and in the spiritual enrichment both of the Sovereign and the people. "The clouds drop the dew."

> Ye fearful saints, fresh courage take,
> The clouds ye so much dread
> Are big with mercy, and shall break
> With blessings on your head.[1]

And so I have thought it might be calming and cheering if I thus direct your meditations to the ministry of the cloud. Have you ever noticed how many of the dispositions of the perfected life can only be richly gained in the baptism of shadow and tears? We are accustomed to speak of them as the fruits and flowers of the Spirit. I sometimes think we might be nearer the truth if we spoke of them as the ferns. Flowers are suggestive of the sunny glare; ferns are more significant of the moistened shade. And when I contemplate the dispositions which are the creations of the Spirit, I feel that for their

---

1 A quote from *God Moves in a Mysterious Way* by William Cowper.

perfect nourishing something is needed of moistness and of shade. Here is a short list of the beautiful things: "Love, joy, peace, long-suffering, gentleness, goodness, meekness, temperance, faith." I say, I am more inclined to call them ferns than flowers! I don't think they would come to any luxuriant profusion and beauty if they were grown in the prolonged and cloudless glare! They need not only the upward calling of the light, but the feeding baptism of waters and the restfulness of the shade.

Here is an exquisite fern—"gentleness." Where will you find it growing in richest profusion? You will find it growing in the life that has known the shadow and the tear. There is no touch so tenderly gentle as the touch of the wounded hand. There is no speech so insinuatingly sympathetic as the speech of those who have been folded about by the garment of night. Gentleness is a fern, and it requires the ministry of the cloud. Here is another rare and beautiful fern—"long-suffering." How can you grow that in the "garish day"! You may as well plant out your ferns in the middle of the unprotected lawn, and let the fierce darts of light strike upon them through the long day, and expect to have a mass of broad, healthy, graceful fronds, as expect to find "long-suffering" flourishing where there is no shadow of trial, no chill of darkness and tears. "Long-suffering" is a fern, and it needs the ministry of the cloud. And is it otherwise with the ferns of "goodness" and "love"? How this love-fern expands when life passes into the shadow; when husband or child is laid low, how love puts on strength and beauty, whether the lover be peasant-wife or queen! When I remember these things, when I recall the purpose of all living, to make perfectly holy our dispositions, I do not wonder that, for the sake of the fern-like qualities of the spirit, we are sometimes taken out of the brightness of "the green pastures" into "the valley of the shadow," and are put under the gracious influence of the ministry of the cloud.

Now, I do not think we have any difficulty in perceiving the influence of the cloud in the individual life. Perhaps we may find its best expression in the familiar words of the Psalmist, "In my distress Thou hast enlarged me."[1] Enlarged! It is a very spacious word, and includes the complementary meanings of broadening

---

1 See Psalm 4:1.

and enrichment. "In my cloud-experience Thou hast enriched me!" Some little languishing fern of tenderness or thoughtfulness has been revived by the ministry of the moistened shade. Is that an altogether unfamiliar experience? A man goes into the cloud rough and boorish, and full of domineering aggression, and he emerges from its ministry strangely softened and refined! He entered the cloud hard and dry as a pavement; he emerges with disposition suggestive of the fernery. "In my distress Thou hast enriched me!"

The cloud experience is the minister not only of enrichment, but of enlargement. It is in the cloud that men grow the fern of a spacious tolerance. Narrowness is transformed to breadth. I have known a man of very stern, severe, and rigid creed, who definitely relegated to damnation all who lived beyond its sharp and imprisoning fence; and I have met him again in after years, and I found that the barbed wire was down, and the field of his sympathy was immeasurably enlarged. "But that is not what you used to believe ten years ago?" "No, but many things have happened since then." Then I learned that he had been in the valley of the shadow! Adversity had wrapped him in its clammy embrace! He had become very familiar with the grave; the way to the cemetery was well worn by his accustomed feet; he had been under the tuition and ministry of the cloud, and in his distress he had been enlarged! The clouds had dropped their dew! In the personal life, if it were not for the cloud we should become and remain dry and infertile as the Sahara; it is the providential cloud that calls forth the hidden growth, the sleeping ferns, and transforms the dust-heap into a thing of grace and beauty.

It is not otherwise with the ministry of the cloud in the sphere of the home. There is many a family which never realizes its unity until it is enveloped in the folds of a chilling cloud. Health and luxury are too often divisive; sickness and sorrow are wondrous cements. Luxury nourishes a thoughtless individualism; adversity discovers hidden and profounder kinships. There is many a home, whose light has been as the glitter and the dazzle of a garish day; and the daughters of the house have been the creatures of levity and flippancy and of an endless trifling. And the cloud has come, and gloom has filled the house; the father is stricken, and adversity shows its famine-teeth at the door; and these flippant daughters awake from their luxurious sleep, and they put on moral strength and beauty like a robe. The family has found its unity in its distress. "We shall know each other better when the mists have rolled away!" Ah! but we sometimes never know each other until we meet together in the mist! It is in the common cloud that the family finds its kinship. It is in our sorrow that deep calleth unto deep, and our communion is revealed.

Is it otherwise in the larger life and family of the nations? Does the cloud-ministry exercise its influence in the State? Surely we may say that the common life of a people is deepened and enriched by the ministry of the shade. A people is not consolidated by common material interests and aims. It is not by free trade or by reciprocity that we shall forge the links of enduring fellowships. These ties are only skin-ties, and they are the subjects of skin disease. Juxtaposition is not fellowship. You may place men in a common schedule and yet not make them more akin. Men may march together without being agreed. We may revise our commercial relationships, and yet the springs of unity may not be touched. We shall never owe our deepened fellowship to the dazzle; we shall owe it to the shade. It is not the prosperous glare that makes us one. We fall apart in the noontide; we draw closer to each other in the night. It is in the national clouds and shadows, and in the nation's tears that you will find the forces of a true consolidation. It is not in the nation's shout, but in the nation's hush that the unifying forces are at work. There has been a marvellous growth in the mutual attachment of sovereign and people during the last twenty-five or thirty years. Has the cloud had any share in the enrichment? Even twenty-five years ago there was a broad republican sentiment prevalent in the nation. It was shared by some who now occupy exalted positions of state. In our own day it has weakened almost to the point of extinction. It is rarely, if ever, whispered in the broad plains of public life. How is the change to be explained? Instinctively we think of the late Queen's goodness, of her sane and healthy judgment, of her unfailing tact and discretion, of her single-minded devotion to her subjects' weal. And certainly all these were forces of integration, but having named them is the situation now explained? I confess to you that much

as I esteemed Queen Victoria's mental and spiritual resources, it is
not to her endowments but to her sorrows that I would point if I
wished to find the primary causes of this deepened attachment and
regard. I think her clouded experiences accomplished as much as
her sovereign gifts, and that in the sharing of common sorrow monarch and people approached in ever deeper and richer communion.
It was not by the passing of imperial pageants that the welding was
effected, but by the so-often repeated passing of the funeral train as
it made its somber journey from the palace to the grave! No, not by
the dazzling splendor of her sovereignty, but by the grey and sober
ministry of the cloud, revealing the kindred humanness of monarch
and people, and in its vital depths creating the mutual bonds of lov-
ing and reverent attachment.

The clouds, in their courses, have been the friends of the
national life.

Chapter 26

THE REALMS OF THE BLEST

And so shall we ever be with the Lord.—1 Thessalonians 4:17.

I want to turn your attention to that blessed land in which our Saviour rules as King, and where our departed have ceaseless communion with Him. I know it is out of fashion to meditate about heaven. It is regarded as somewhat effeminate even to speak of the abodes of the blessed. I suppose it partly arises from what is regarded as a very healthy disparagement of mere emotion and sentiment. It seems to be commonly thought that people who ponder much upon heaven have their fiber softened and their faculties generally debilitated and impaired.

I remember that when I first came out of college, and took up the work of the Christian ministry, I fervently shared this common belief, and I felt with a good many other young reformers that instead of singing about the things of the blessed and the doings of the eternal life, I would engage the interest of my congregation in the condition of the slums, and the uncleanness of the common streets of our own city. Rather than waste sentiment and thought upon the life that is to be, I would seek to concentrate all our energy in bettering the life that is.

I think I have learned a larger lesson. I have discovered that no man works less eagerly in the slums, because now and again he has a view of the City of God, and no man has a softened fiber because he stimulates his imagination in trying to realize the life that is to be. What kind of power does it impair? What kind of faculty does it soften, to think occasionally about the land to which we are all has-tening? Does it soften the will? Does it in any way bedim the con-science? Does it narrow or strain the affections? Let us be definite in our charge, let us seek to put our finger upon that particular part of our mental or spiritual constitution which is in any way injured by the steady, frequent, regular contemplation of the Eternal Rest. In what way does it unfit men for practical life? In what way does it create dreamers? "I should like to meet with a few of these dreamy people," says Faber, "first to be sure of the fact, which I venture to doubt, and secondly to be sure I should condemn their dreaminess, which I doubt also."

Well, now, suppose we do give a little of our time to thought about the better land, and the Lord of the better land, what may we hope to accomplish by it? I have been lately spending a very busy week among the saints, that I might discover from their experi-ence what they have found from such contemplation. What do they find? Here is a quaint phrase in which one of the saints expresses his sense of the value of heavenly meditation. "It will prevent a shyness between thy soul and God." Love is exquisitely shy, and our love for our Saviour has, I think, in its beginning, just this little touch of shyness which wears away as we engage in frequent talk and com-munion with Him.

What else have the saints found in heavenly contemplation? Here is Richard Baxter's answer: "It will open the door between thy head and thy heart," and then he goes on to say, in what I consider a very suggestive phrase: "He is usually the best Christian who has the readiest passage from his brain to his heart." Do you see the significance of that? We take into our minds a certain truth, a cer-tain mental conception; if we meditate upon the truth received, the ministry of meditation transfers the truth from the mind to the affections. It becomes more than a mental apprehension; it becomes a part of our love. It turns a thing of the brain into a power of the life. It begins to energise the passions, waking them, feeding them, nourishing those parts of our life which are the most potent in determining our activity.

What else will it accomplish? It will bring the needed inspira-tion in times of temptation and distress. "When should we take our cordial," says our friend the Puritan, "but in times of fainting?" When the tempter is very near you, or when distress seems to overwhelm you like a flood—then is one of the seasons when you ought to turn your mind to the land of the blessed, because from that contemplation there will come nutriment and inspiration by which you shall be sustained in your darkest hour and carried through in safety. Now that is most characteristic of Samuel Rutherford. I confess that when I am reading one of his letters, and I find that he is dealing with some season of distress, some season of overwhelming tribulation, I almost welcome it because I know he will bring out some of the heavenly counsel and experience which he has acquired in season of communion with God. "I had rather," he says, "I had rather have Christ's buffet and Christ's love stroke than any king's kiss." He weighs his pain over against the coming glory. In the hour of his sorrow he meditates upon the coming bliss, and the contemplation of the bliss transfigures the present sorrow.

Find out the best place whence you can send your thoughts heavenward. Richard Baxter said that he always found that his "fattest time" was in the evening, from the sunset to the twilight. It may not be your best time, it may not be your convenient time; but find a place and find an hour when you can send your imagination among the realms of the blessed, to remind yourselves of the country towards which you are going, of the inheritance to whose possession you are succeeding, and give yourself the sense of the dignity of one who has part and lot in the matter, who is a partaker of the Divine nature, and will share with the Eternal the blessedness of eternity.

What are some of the characteristic glories of the life which is to be spent for ever with the Lord? I can tell you nothing you do not know; but perhaps just by repeating a commonplace in a fresh way I may give it a certain newness.

It is a life of rest. I do not wonder that Faber, in one of his books, when he had mentioned this word "rest," added the sentence: "Let us stay and suck that word as if it were a honeycomb." Now people who are never tired cannot know the significance of rest. But people who have to labor very hard, and amid very straitened circumstances, find in the word a delicious consolation. I remember once talking with a fisher-woman who had lost her husband and two sons at sea, away down in Cullercoats Bay on the Northumberland coast. I asked her what she liked most to think about when she thought about the land beyond, and I was not surprised to hear her say, "And there shall be no more sea." And when you go to very tired people, people who are not only physically tired but mentally worn, there is no word which appeals to them with such sweet significance as just this common word "rest." I said to one of my people the other day, as I stood by his dying bed: "Rest comes at length!" And the tired eyes lit up, and I knew the meaning of the expectancy that leaped into his hungry eyes. "They shall hunger no more, neither thirst any more, neither shall the sun light upon them nor any heat";[1] "there shall be no more pain."[2]

It is a life of quest. It is not a life of mere passivity, but a life of glorious activity. First of all our quest is to be under the immediate leadership of our Lord: "He shall lead them to living fountains of water."[3] The unveiling of new things, the unsealing of new springs! When we have dropped the clay and the veil of the flesh, we shall stand out with immeasurably increased powers of perception, and going with our Lord as our personal conductor among the wonders of unveiled truth and all the splendors of glory, with our immeasurably intensified powers, we shall find countless kinds of new and unimaginable delights break out before us on every side.

It is a life of service. I like that little phrase that Swedenborg uses—and among all the apparent fictions and fancies and flimsy conceits of Swedenborgianism you sometimes come across what you feel at once to be rare gems of superlative truth—Swedenborg says concerning the employments of heaven: "There will be occupation but no labor." The worker is never tired! His activity is never toil! It is a life of uses, and every soul will have its individual enterprise.

And it is a life of wondrous communion. First of all, it is communion with one another. I sometimes say to my people when they are telling me their sorrows and their troubles, and when neither the teller nor the hearer can find even the faintest clue, "You will explain it to me some day!" I say it as a glorious conviction that one

---

1 Revelation 7:16.
2 Revelation 21:4.
3 Revelation 7:17.

of the joys and delights of the heavenly country will be the perfect understanding of the things that have bewildered us here. We shall get the clue, and we shall tell one another the story which down here we found a burden and a destroyer of our peace.

But the joy of fellowship will be not only fellowship one with another, but fellowship with those spirits who "have never, never known a fallen world like this." If you were to ask me to put my finger upon one page in all the published writings of Dr. Dale which is written most deeply on my mind and heart, it would be that glorious passage in which he is expounding this great word to the Ephesians: "to the principalities and powers in the heavenly place there shall be made known the manifold wisdom of God."[1] Dr. Dale speaks about the redeemed pilgrims of time telling the inhabitants of the heavenly city who have never known our estate, who have never known our sin, the story of redemption, and of how our hunger was met and how our peace was renewed; and they will tell the pilgrims about the unclouded day, about the far-away time when sin had not fallen upon the world, and all about the wonderful developments and experiences of the unsullied life.

But pre-eminently, and above all other things, *it is to be a life of fellowship with the Lord*. "For ever with the Lord! Amen, so let it be!"[2] "The Lamb which is in the midst of the throne shall tabernacle among them."[3] It is a homely figure; it is the figure of a meeting-place of many tents, and our God comes and adds His tent to the number. He is one with us, one among us; allowing us to go into His tent, and coming into our tent, a life of shared fellowship, a life of close intimacy in the things of the blessed.

Well, now, let us give a little time to thinking about these things. In twelve months' time some of us will probably be in the heavenly country. Surely it is well just to think a little about the glories and beauties of the land. "Half-an-hour in heaven," said a working man to me one day, "half-an-hour in heaven and I am ready for anything!" Spend a little time with the Lord now, and you will be prepared to spend the *"forever* with the Lord." Amen.

---

1 Ephesians 3:10.

2 A quote from *Forever with the Lord* by James Montgomery.

3 See Revelation 7:17.

Printed in Great Britain
by Amazon

18369804R00082